IS THE FETUS
HUMAN?

IS THE FETUS HUMAN?

By
Eric J. Pastuszek
and Robert B. French

TAN BOOKS AND PUBLISHERS, INC.
Rockford, Illinois 61105

TAN BOOKS AND PUBLISHERS, INC.
P.O. Box 424
Rockford, Illinois 61105
1993

To Jesus,
Who Was Once a Fetus.

Even if man, denying all evidence of life within the womb, attempts to label the fetus as nothing more than a mere "blob," the fact remains that the fetus is a unique form of life that one day will fully develop into a unique adult. Once that fetus is destroyed, that unique adult will never exist. And how many great statesmen, architects, men of God, scientists—even doctors—has our world lost to abortion?

Contents

The Rule Against Perpetuities (an inheritance/estate law).

Acknowledgments

I am grateful to countless people and organizations who have contributed to this book. I heartily express thanks to all of you who helped.

In regard to permission for reprinting material, I acknowledge the following:

Australian and New Zealand Journal of Psychiatry, "The Foetus as a Personality," by A. W. Liley, June 1972.

Abortion. . .Questions and Answers by Dr. John Willke, Hayes Publishing Company, 1985. With permission.

Operation Rescue by Randall Terry, copyright 1988. Used by permission of the publisher, Whitaker House, Pittsburgh and Colfax Sts., Springdale, PA 15144.

Rites of Life by Landrum Shettles, M.D., and David Rorvik. Copyright 1983 by Landrum B. Shettles, M.D., and David Rorvik. Used by permission of Zondervan Publishing House.

Larson's Book of Family Issues by Bob Larson, copyright 1986 Bob Larson, used by permission of Tyndale House Publishers, Inc. All rights reserved.

A Private Choice: Abortion in America in the Seventies by John T. Noonan, Jr. Copyright 1979 by The Free Press, a Division of Macmillan, Inc. Reprinted by permission of the publisher.

Aborting America by Bernard Nathanson, M.D., Doubleday & Company, Inc., copyright 1979 by Bernard Nathanson.

The Catholic Catechism by John Hardon, Doubleday & Company, Inc., 1975.

Foreword

"The argument over whether the unborn child is human or not has been bogus from the start. If it is not human, what is it, a Buick? Eric Pastuszek offers us convincing evidence for those still interested in facts that the unborn child is not only human, but is deserving of the protection of law it once enjoyed."

—Cal Thomas
Syndicated Columnist

Preface

The researchers of this work conducted an independent study by collecting, analyzing, and validating various evidence concerning the fetus. The scientific definition of the fetus pertains to the developing embryo from twelve weeks gestation to birth. The evidence within this book covers human development from conception through birth. On the strict biological forefront, several ex-abortionists present their candid view of the abortion process. In addition, photographs of aborted fetuses, seldom shown in the press, are presented. Other evidence unveiled includes a personal interview with a woman who had an abortion, the commercial and scientific use of the fetus, and rising civil disobedience in support of the unborn.

Biblical quotes and religious citations are also included in this work. A wide range of religious views is shown, including a look at how Protestantism views the fetus.

Although many will not accept biblical and religious evidence on the humanity of the fetus, it is presented alongside the tangible biological and medical facts because of the tremendous religious influence in our culture.

Introduction

A beating heart at 18 days; a still-life picture of a whole fetus, with eyelashes, even fingernails, aborted at 24 weeks; testimonies of ex-abortionists—these are but a few samples of the tremendous evidence that compels us to ask: Is the fetus human?

On January 22, 1973, the U.S. Supreme Court legalized abortion virtually on demand through all nine months of pregnancy for the United States in *Roe v. Wade* (410 US 113 [1973]). That ruling struck down a majority of state laws that outlawed or severely restricted abortion. (The Supreme Court did allow states the option of barring third-trimester abortions—those in the last three months of pregnancy—except to save the life of the mother.) However, the verdict to allow abortion virtually on demand throughout pregnancy did not consider biological and other facts pertaining to the humanity of the fetus. Evidence showed that the fetus inside the womb was a definable, unique human being. Since the *Roe v. Wade* decision, even more evidence has been produced, due to advancing technology, such as the fetoscope, which makes it possible to view the fetus within the womb.

Neither the legislative branch nor the judiciary branch (i.e., Supreme Court) of the U.S. government has addressed the question, "Is the fetus human?" If the fetus is human, abortion on demand is wrong—unless our society forsakes all ethics and allows murder. Only if the fetus is not human may the law allow it to be aborted.

Throughout the past decade, especially in the late 1980s, efforts have focused on restricting abortion. Court decisions and legislation, while somewhat successful with restrictions, have still failed to address the question that *Roe v. Wade*'s author, Justice Blackmun, sidestepped in 1973—the question of the humanity of the fetus.

Federal regulations (on fetal experimentation, for example) have not been enough to define at what stage life must receive legal protection; the legal issue of abortion on demand may only be settled when an objective, non-biased, honest court assesses each week of fetal development and stipulates the periods of pregnancy during which the fetus is human.

Abortion on demand through all nine months of pregnancy never existed in the United States until 1973. In fact, the American Medical Association initially rejected the notion of abortion on demand. State laws began to change, due to pressure from fringe social groups, in the 1950's and 1960's. However, not until January 22, 1973, did the United States allow nationwide abortion on demand through virtually all nine months of pregnancy.

Not only did early Christianity reject the notion of abortion on demand, even some pre-Christian societies forbade it. Both Judaism and Christianity have protected the fetus by declaring abortion to be murder. The Hippocratic Oath, taken by some physicians even today, expressly rejects abortion. Modern physicians have modified the Hippocratic Oath to eliminate the prohibition of abortion.

One may ask, "If the fetus is human, why don't we see the evidence?" Most abortionists would prefer to hide it. Generally, fetuses are incinerated after abortion, although a group in Milwaukee gathered 5,000 little fetuses (bodies with hands, feet, etc.) and arranged a 100-car funeral procession to bury them. The Milwaukee incident is only one case in which the physical remains of abortion were exposed. A similar case occurred in Woodland Hills, California, where 16,433 fetuses were uncovered by workers emptying a storage container. The book entitled *The Woodland Hills Tragedy* described this incident.

Since 1973, America has legally aborted more than 25 million fetuses without resolving the crucial question, "Is the fetus human?" The answer to this question is often based upon whether the fetus is wanted by its biological mother. A medical doctor performing an abortion because of an unwanted pregnancy may reject the evidence that the fetus is human.

However, sometimes simultaneously, a medical researcher will request a fetus for experimentation because the fetus provides a much-needed "human" specimen, as opposed to the animals (for example, mice) typically used in research. Meanwhile, medical technology, such as ultrasound, adds to the medical evidence on the life of the tiny beings in the womb.

Within these pages is the evidence—biological, medical, emotional, legal, cultural and social. Examine the evidence and answer for yourself: Is the fetus human?

1

Biological Evidence

(Note: The following question and answer are from an interview with Carol Everett, who formerly owned two abortion clinics and operated two abortion clinics. See also p. 14.)

Q: *"During conversations within the clinic, would you or your colleagues ever refer to the aborted being as a boy or girl, or a baby?"*

A: "We never referred to a boy or a girl. We referred to a baby. We would say, 'How many babies are we going to kill today?' "

A distinct heartbeat, unique human genetic makeup, the ability to move, to hear sounds, and even to detect light—these are some of the many biological aspects of the fetus within the womb. A heartbeat can be detected as early as 18 days. Genetic makeup (for example, 46 chromosomes—the unique genetic scheme for each adult) exists within the fetus from conception. The fetus begins moving during the first trimester; visual and auditory senses are developed at various stages during pregnancy. The fetus even develops a sense of pain.

The topics discussed within this chapter are:

Biology and Fetology
Basic Biological Facts About the Fetus
The Genetic Makeup of the Fetus
Scientific Evidence of Human Life Within the Womb
Statements From Ex-abortionists

1.1 Biology and Fetology

Biological evidence concerning the fetus certainly existed prior to the twentieth century. Biological evidence in this study refers to scientific, medical and other facts that bear on the question of whether the fetus is human. A former abortionist wrote that "the nineteenth century produced a number of biological advances that undoubtedly affected doctors' opinions on what was moral in abortion. The idea that intrauterine life began at 'quickening' [when the woman first feels the fetus move] was eroded by the newly invigorated field of embryology that expanded after Von Baer reported the first visualization of a mammalian ovum in 1827."[1]

The modern biological evidence amassed recently is also compelling. For example, U.S. Supreme Court Justice Sandra Day O'Connor wrote, "As medical science becomes better able to provide for the separate existence of the fetus, the point of viability is moved further back toward conception."[2] "Viability" is the ability of the fetus to survive outside the womb, a situation now reached in the middle months of pregnancy, thanks to medical advances that allow babies to survive earlier and earlier premature births.

The field of fetology is one example of the current investigation of life in the womb. The fetoscope, a camera that takes pictures of the fetus in the womb, now enables us to view life before birth.

1.2 Basic Biological Facts About the Fetus

Some of the elementary biological facts about the fetus (which in Latin means "young one") are the following:

The heart begins beating as early as the 18th day.

The structure for the entire nervous system exists by the 20th day.

At 42 days, the skeleton is complete; reflexes are present.

The brain and all body systems are present by eight weeks.

At eight weeks, if the fetus' nose is tickled, he will flex his head backwards, away from the stimulus.

At nine to ten weeks, the fetus squints, swallows and moves his tongue; if you stroke his palm, he will make a fist.

At 11 to 12 weeks, he sucks his thumb vigorously and breathes the amniotic fluid to develop the organs of respiration.

Fingernails are present by 11 to 12 weeks, eyelashes by 16 weeks.

The fetus moves within the womb before the mother feels movement.

All body systems are functioning by 12 weeks.

The fetus has a blood supply separate from the mother's blood supply.

Other biological facts (reported by writer Melody Green) are the following: The fetus "moves his arms and legs by six weeks, and by 43 days his brain waves can be read."[3] "By eight weeks the baby has his very own fingerprints, he can urinate, make a strong fist, and he can feel pain. Each stage of development from fertilization to old age is merely a maturing of what is entirely there at the start."[4]

Another author, Bob Larson, provided further information on the fetus' early development.

> Within a week [after conception], the vertebrae, spine, and nervous system form, and the kidneys, liver and digestive system begin to grow. By the eighteenth day, a primitive heart pumps its own blood. At thirty days, nubbins of limbs appear. The skeleton is complete at a month and a half, and its first movements are made. At five weeks, the brain divides into its three parts and grows rapidly. The eight-week-old fetus is barely an inch long and most of its internal organs are in place. The baby can grasp objects, swim, hiccup, suck its thumb, wake, and sleep with regularity.[5]

Furthermore, he stated, "At the eleven-week stage, all body systems are formed and functioning."[6]

Although not fully developed, the fetus can be compared to a two-year-old child. The young child's bones, for example, have not fully developed; likewise the fetus, while containing all its body parts, is in the process of development.

1.3 The Genetic Makeup of the Fetus

Despite claims by some scientists that the fetus or embryo can be compared to a fish or tadpole, the fetus most closely resembles a human because of the very human organs that scientists themselves harvest for admittedly *human* experimentation (See Section 1.8). The fetus is a unique biological entity that, like a child, is not yet fully grown; however, each person contains the same genetic makeup from his conception through adulthood.

A fetal cell contains the same number of chromosomes as the cell of an adult, and chromosomes contain the unique genetic characteristics that determine what each human being will be. Each normal healthy human being has a set of 46 chromosomes. There are exceptions: for example, a Down's Syndrome child has 47 chromosomes.

In an article entitled "Human Life Begins at Conception," Landrum B. Shettles, M.D., and David Rorvik verified the genetic evidence that the cell of a fetus contains the same number of chromosomes as the cell of an adult. Dr. Shettles "first discovered and distinguished between male and female producing sperm, and he continues to pioneer research in [the field of] in vitro fertilization."[7] Their article can be summarized as follows:

> The Nature of Cells in a Human
> The Merger of a Male and Female Sex Cell (Conception)
> The Fetus as a Distinct Human Life

The Nature of Cells in a Human

Soma (Greek for "body") *Cells*: Most of the billions of cells that exist in a human are "soma cells"; these cells make up the skin, organs, muscle, etc.[8]

Sex Cells (male and female reproductive cells, i.e., sperm and ovum): "There are some other, far rarer cells, however, known as 'germ' cells or 'sex' cells " or "gametes " that exist within the male and female. When a sex cell of a male unites with that of a female, a new human life is conceived.[9]

Chromosomes. Each type of cell, either a soma cell or a sex cell, contains chromosomes, forming a blueprint that defines each unique human being's characteristics. An interesting fact here is that each soma cell typically contains 46 chromosomes, whereas each sex cell has 23 chromosomes. "It is only through combination, through merger, that the sex cells attain the full complement of hereditary units that defines a human being."[10]

Merger of a Male and a Female Reproductive Cell (Conception)

Conception. Conception occurs when a male sex cell unites with a female sex cell. A "zygote" forms. A zygote, unlike a single sex cell (male or female), is a unique human entity.[11]

Uniqueness. Each conception produces a unique human being because "the genotype—the inherited characteristics of a unique human being—is established in the conception process and will remain in force for the entire life of that individual. No other event in biological life is so decisive as this one; no other set of circumstances can even remotely rival genotype in 'making you what you are.' "[12] Shettles and Rorvik stated:

> Conception confers life and makes that life one of a kind. Unless you have an identical twin, there is virtually no chance, in the natural course of things, that there will be "another you"—not even if mankind were to persist for billions of years.[13]

Bob Larson wrote of the uniqueness of each conception:

> At conception, a new and totally different human being exists with forty-six chromosomes (the same as any human) and the capability of replacing its own dying cells.[14]

Modern medical textbooks also confirm that a unique individual results from conception:

> Thus a new cell is formed from the union of a male and a female gamete. The cell, referred to as the *zygote,* contains a new combination of genetic material, resulting in an individual different from either parent and from anyone else in the world.[15]

The Fetus as a Distinct Human Life

Chromosomes Fixed Through Adulthood. Whether the fetus is newly conceived (a zygote) or in its eighth week, the unique biological chromosomes remain the same; they do not change from one's conception through adulthood. "Whatever the terminology, the unborn is *always* a distinct entity, an individual human life in its own right," wrote Shettles and Rorvik.[16]

The Fetus Supervises the Pregnancy. "Fetologist Albert W. Liley has asserted: 'It is the fetus who is in charge of the pregnancy.' Even some who oppose restrictions on abortion would readily agree. For example, Daniel Callahan, director of the Institute of Society, Ethics and the Life Sciences, has stated: 'Genetically, hormonally and in all organic respects, save for the source of its nourishment, a fetus and even an embryo is separate from the woman...' "[17]

In conclusion, based on genetic evidence, such as stated above, an honest and objective assessment of the genetic makeup of the fetus indicates that the fetus is a new human being whose cells carry the same unique chromosomes, i.e., the same blueprint, from conception through adulthood.

1.4 Scientific Evidence of Human Life Within the Womb

Dr. Bernard Nathanson, a former abortionist, stated that "hardly anyone in the medical community still openly denies that the pre-born child is a biological human."[18] Dr. Nathanson mentioned that, due to medical advances in the early 1970s, a biological window into the womb was evolving. He summarized this development as follows:

> In the early 70s we began to use machinery, apparatus, and instruments which allowed us to finally put a larger and much more sophisticated window into the womb. But for the first time as a physician and as an ethical person, I began to understand that more was involved in an abortion than merely suctioning out a mass of cells, a few grams of tissue. I began to be aware that there was something here which had a moral density to it which commanded respect. [19]

Nathanson also stated, "There is no longer serious doubt in my mind that human life exists within the womb from the very onset of pregnancy."[20]

Dr. Hymie Gordon's testimony confirms Nathanson's belief that the fetus is more than a "few grams of tissue." Dr. Gordon, Chairman of the Department of Medical Genetics at the Mayo Clinic, stated in his testimony before the U.S. Senate that "by the criteria of modern molecular biology, life is present from the moment of conception."[21]

Perhaps the most striking admission came from an article in *California Medicine* in 1971; it stated that, as a result of inventing new terminology such as "terminating a pregnancy," instead of "killing a baby," there "has been a curious avoidance of the scientific fact, which everyone really knows, that human life begins at conception and is continuous whether intra- or extra-uterine until death."[22]

Equally striking are the words of Dr. Alan Guttmacher, late president of Planned Parenthood, who stated in his book, *Planning Your Family,* that a "new life" begins at fertilization.[23]

One physician, citing excellent biological evidence of the fetus' humanity, stated:

> Eleven years ago while giving an anesthetic for a ruptured ectopic pregnancy (at two months gestation) I was handed what I believed was the smallest living human ever seen. The embryo sac was intact and transparent. Within the sac

was a tiny human male swimming vigorously in the amniotic fluid, while attached to the wall by the umbilical cord. This tiny human was perfectly developed, with long, tapering fingers, feet, and toes. It was almost transparent, as regards the skin, and the delicate arteries and veins were prominent to the ends of the fingers.

The baby was extremely alive and swam about the sac approximately one time per second, with a natural swimmer's stroke. This tiny human did not look at all like the photos and drawings and models of "embryos" which I have seen, nor did it look like a few embryos I have been able to observe since then, obviously because this one was alive!

...When the sac was opened, the tiny human immediately lost its life and took on the appearance of what is accepted as the appearance of an embryo at this stage (blunt extremities, etc.). It is my opinion that if the lawmakers, and people realized that very vigorous life is present, it is possible that abortion would be found more objectionable than euthanasia.[24]

Perhaps the most convincing scientific evidence came with the development of the fetoscope in the 1980s, a highly advanced microscope that produces fiberoptic images of the fetus inside the womb. Until a few years ago, the fiberoptic images were impossible to produce. Let us look at the following narration of the vivid detail shown from inside the womb during a television segment:

So many decisions for abortion are based on the "out of sight, out of mind" reasoning, not fully understanding what is really taking place or ever visualizing the child that is maturing in the sanctuary of the mother's womb. But, through the use of a highly sophisticated microscope called a fetoscope, we can see this little baby beginning his growing adventure in life...this little fellow is only weeks old...but just a few years ago, these fiberoptic images were impossible to produce.

Note the blood vessels running under the delicate skin, the hand and the fingers. This thick, blue coiled structure is the umbilical cord. This is the child's lifeline to the mother. This is a little boy. The ear is readily identifiable. It has been shown that in the later months of pregnancy the child will react to sound. There is the nose...the mouth. This little fellow can even be seen swallowing water. The eyebrows. And the eyelids are still closed.

Tragically, what you are watching is dramatic footage of preparation images for an abortion by dismemberment which abruptly ended this child's life. I simply cannot show you the rest of this gruesome film. The visual details of this less than eight minute procedure are inappropriate for television viewing. These scenes are excerpts from the film *Eclipse of Reason*...a startling look at the reality of abortion. The conclusion of that abortion procedure produced a bloody pile of rubble, destroying this young boy's life.

Abortion is clearly the taking of a human life. Many have tried to dismiss the obvious scientific evidence of life's existence from the point of conception by using an approach which is the equivalent of a theory that the earth is flat. Through the discoveries of today's medical science and technology, the understanding of life at conception is more vivid than ever before.[25]

The man known as the Father of Fetology, A. W. Liley, made great contributions to our understanding of life in the womb. Of particular importance here is his article entitled "The Foetus as a Personality." Author Suzanne M. Rini described his work:

With...simple tools, A. W. Liley, who died in 1983, explored the world of the fetus in utero. From his journeys with simple instruments, he concluded not that the fetus is a *tabula rasa* [blank slate] or a tadpole, a subhuman or an alien, foreigner, but said with never diminishing wonder that fetal life is conscious, alert to learning and stimuli, already both a person and a patient. It is indeed significant that A. W. Liley delivered [his] address ["The Foetus as a Personality"] to his colleagues on the eve of the abortion decision in Australia. It was a noble attempt to universalize at the moment when all was about to become relative and saleable.[26]

Community myth, based on societal ignorance, depicts the fetus as an inactive entity; even some scientists, in denial of the tremendous evidence within fetology alone, blatantly attempt to misconstrue the fetus as a fish or a tadpole. However, A. W. Liley was one of many scientists who clearly provided immense evidence that the fetus is a conscious, alert member of the human race. A. W. Liley's article, "The Foetus as a Personality," yields these scientific facts about the fetus:

> The fetus controls the pregnancy.
> The fetus is conscious (for example, it moves as early as eight weeks).
> The fetus is alert.
> The fetus sees.
> The fetus hears.

Many people believe that the fetus is an "inert passenger." Nothing could be further from the scientific truth. A. W. Liley refused "conjecture" about the fetus and stated the following based on his scientific studies:

> If, with regret, we must abandon such fascinating conjecture, I hope that we can replace it with equally interesting fact, because recent advances in foetal diagnosis and therapy have provided both the technology and opportunity to piece together a new picture of the foetus. Far from being an inert passenger in a pregnant mother, the foetus is very much in command of the pregnancy. It is the foetus who guarantees the endocrine success of the pregnancy and induces all manner of changes in maternal physiology to make her a suitable host. It is the foetus who, single-handedly, solves the homograft problem—no mean feat when we reflect that, biologically, it is quite possible for a woman to bear more than her own body weight of babies, all immunological foreigners, during her reproductive career. It is the foetus who determines the duration of pregnancy. It is the foetus who decides which way he will lie in pregnancy and which way he will present [himself] in labour.[27]

Most importantly, A. W. Liley's studies are based on medical advances that provide an accurate picture of the fetus. For example, the fetus can be described as a conscious being. Liley affirmed this:

> In his warm and humid microclimate, the foetus is in neither stupor nor hypoxic coma. From the few electroencephalographic studies, he appears to show cyclical activity, the lighter periods which correspond in the neonate to a drowsy wakefulness from which he is readily aroused by a variety of stimuli. Like all internal organs, the uterus is insensitive to touch, indeed, to all stimuli except stretch. Hence foetal movements are not felt in the uterus but in the maternal abdominal wall, which explains why quickening is not apparent until 16 to 22 weeks of gestation. The foetus has been moving his limbs and trunk since about 8 weeks, but some 10 or more weeks elapse before these movements are strong enough to be transmitted to the abdominal wall.[28]

Biological evidence within the womb also reveals that the fetus is alert. For example, the fetus rolls over (using the spine), determines his or her position in the womb (or for birth), and responds to pressure and touch. Dr. Liley stated these facts:

> The mechanism by which the foetus changes ends in the uterus is simple—he propels himself around by his feet and legs. The mechanism by which he changes sides is more subtle—he employs an elegant longitudinal spiral roll and at the midpoint of his turn has a 180° twist in his spine.
> ...he can assume postures difficult or impossible for the child or adult...
> The foetus is responsive to pressure and touch. Tickling the foetal scalp at surgical induction of labor provokes movement, stroking the palm of a prolapsed arm elicits a grasp reflex, and to plantar stimulation the footling breech obliges with an upgoing toe.[29]

Dr. Liley also noted that the fetus swallows amniotic fluid and experiences hiccups. These and other facts indicate that the fetus is indeed conscious and alert, not an inert passenger. His data indicate that the fetus has a profound auditory sense and an existing visual sense. For example, Liley stated:

> ...what the foetus lacks is adequate illumination and a worthwhile image for practice in cone or macular vision. At birth he can see but does not know what he is looking at.[30]

The fetus' sight, while present, is not yet fine-tuned even at birth. Nonetheless, the fetus does have visual capacity within the womb. The following analysis by Liley describes the keen auditory sense of the fetus:

> Sudden noise in a quiet room—the dropping gallipot or maternal voice—startles the foetus lined up under an image intensifier, and from at least 25 weeks the foetus will jump in synchrony with the tympanist's contribution to an orchestral performance.[31]

It is interesting to note that the structures of even the initial fetal inner ear are very close to that of an adult. In addition, the fetus hears internal sounds (within the womb) in addition to external sounds.[32]

In summary, Dr. Liley wrote:

> This then is our picture of the foetus. He does not live in a padded, unchanging cocoon in a state of total sensory deprivation, but in a plastic, reactive structure which buffers and filters, perhaps distorts, but does not eliminate the outside world. Nor is the foetus himself inert and stuporose, but active and responsive.[33]

Some of the best medical evidence confirming Dr. Liley's assertion that the fetus is active and responsive (and not inert) appears in the January 26, 1980 *British Medical Journal* in an article entitled "What the Fetus Feels." The article begins by saying that "the fetus' environment is disturbed by sounds, light, and touch and he responds to these disturbances by moving."[34] This article presents scientific evidence to show that the fetus is an active, responsive being, not simply an "inert" mass of tissue.

The article notes the fetus' acquisition of specific abilities (such as touch) at specific periods of fetal development. As examples of these abilities, the article states:

Sound. "Until the late nineteenth century babies were thought to be born deaf as well as dumb. In fact the inner ear of the fetus is completely developed by mid-pregnancy, and the fetus responds to a wide variety of sounds."[35]

Vision. "Muscles within the orbit are present very early in pregnancy, and the fetus' eyes move when he changes position and during sleep."[36]

Touch. "The fetus can touch parts of his body with his hands and feet, and the umbilical cord also touches all parts of his body."[37]

Spontaneous Movements. "Although the fetus starts making spontaneous movements at about seven weeks after conception, mothers do not usually feel their babies moving until about 16 to 21 weeks."[38]

Pain. "Fetal heart rate and movement increase for a few minutes after tactile stimuli during amniocentesis [Editor's Note: i.e., surgical extraction of fluid from the fetus' amniotic sac]. The fetus then settles down again within a few minutes of the procedure's ending.

"The changes in heart rate and increase in movement suggest that these stimuli are painful for the fetus."[39]

The following list summarizes some statements within the same article that note when an ability is demonstrated by the fetus during a specific gestational age:

Swallowing. At 11 weeks, the fetus swallows surrounding amniotic fluid and passes it back in his urine.[40]

Sound. By mid-pregnancy, loud noises from outside the uterus, such as the slamming of a door or loud music, reach the fetus, who reacts to them.[41]

Touch. By nine weeks, the fetus can bend his fingers around an object in the palm of his hand. At 12 weeks the fetus can close his fingers and thumb and "will open his mouth in response to pressure applied at the base of the thumb."[42]

This biological evidence shows that the fetus has hands, feet, etc., at an early age inside the womb, and that the fetus responds to stimuli (sound, light, touch) at various stages of development. It can even be said that the fetus responds to the emotional stress of its mother. Consider the following statement from the article:

> The fetus' level of activity increases when the mother is under emotional stress. If the stress is prolonged there is a corresponding increase in the fetus' movements—up to 10 times their normal level. The fetus' activity also seems to be increased when the mother is tired.[43]

1.5 Statements From Ex-abortionists

Bernard Nathanson

Dr. Bernard Nathanson, former director of one of the world's largest abortion clinics and one of the founders of the National Abortion Rights Action League, after beginning research in the field of fetology, recanted his earlier pro-abortion views and abandoned his work as an abortionist. He is currently a leading proponent of the right to life for the unborn.

Carol Everett

Carol Everett, who formerly owned two and operated two abortion clinics, was interviewed by the author on Tuesday, April 14, 1989. The following are some of the key questions addressed to Ms. Everett, and her subsequent remarks.

Q: *"Based on your past experience with abortions, would you agree that the fetus is a biological human being?"*

A: "The baby is discernible by the time the woman knows she's pregnant."

Q: *"When does the woman know she's pregnant?"*

A: "About two weeks after she missed her period."

Q: *"Again, based on your experience, did the actual requirements of the certain types of abortions (for example, D & C [dilation and curettage]) entail the necessity of looking for discernible human body parts (e.g., head) in order to complete the abortion? If so, provide specifics."*

A: "You have to have all of the body parts before you can complete the abortion."

Q: *"Would women ever report body parts which remained in the womb?"*

A: "A woman came back at twenty weeks and told us that there was a baby's foot in her womb. I know of other cases when a woman, after having an abortion, would call back and say, 'I just passed a foot' or 'I just passed a hand.' "

Q: *"Were there ever any other fetal movements or fetal expressions (during or after the abortion) which confirmed that the fetus was a human being?"*

A: "You can see the baby moving. When you perform an abortion under sonography, you see the baby move away when the instruments are inserted into the vagina."

Q: *"During conversations within the clinic, would you or your colleagues ever refer to the aborted being as a boy or girl, or a baby?"*

A: "We never referred to a boy or a girl. We referred to a baby. We would say, 'How many babies are we going to kill today?' "

Q: *"Is there any other evidence, particularly biological or medical, from first-hand experience, that you could provide to affirm that the fetus is a human being?"*

A: "They were babies. They all had organs and tissue. I don't know what other evidence you need."

Other ex-abortionists testify about the aborted human body parts that resulted from abortion. (Sometimes the fetus was extracted whole.) Dr. Beverly McMillan, formerly an ardent abortion-rights advocate, stated: "I got to where I just couldn't look at the little bodies anymore."[44]

Dr. Anthony Levatino, who performed abortions as a resident physician at a hospital, said that, while he and his wife were trying to adopt a child, he was "throwing 'em in the garbage at the rate of nine and 10 a week." He finally stopped doing abortions.[45]

Debra Harry, a former abortion assistant in a Michigan clinic, gave instruments to the doctor during the abortion procedure. She recounted hearing the sound of a "baby's skull being crushed."[46] In addition, she said, "I have been there, and I have seen these totally formed babies as early as ten weeks. . .with a leg missing or with their head off. . .I've seen the little rib cages."[47]

1.6 The Remains of Abortion: Body Parts in the Garbage

The statements from ex-abortionists mentioned the body parts pulled from the womb during an abortion. Even after abortion, when the fetal parts become refuse, we see the evidence that even the garbage unveils: bodies at or near the abortion clinics exist in whole, or in part, in the trash dumpsters. The following by Olga Fairfax, Ph.D., is one of the most gripping accounts:

> "Richmond's shame" marked a new low in disposal of wastes. An abortion center there filled a long bin on the rear of its property with the remains of its day's nefarious doings. Its trash compactor neatly mashed 100 babies' bodies which were then tied up in plastic bags and thrown on top of the bin.
>
> The hungry dogs came along and dragged the bags away. There were frequent fights, and the contents of the bags

would be strewn up and down the streets until the dogs
separated the gauze, sponges and pads and devoured the
placenta, bones and flesh of the babies.[48]

Perhaps the most grotesque (yet revealing) incident is known
as the Woodland Hills Tragedy. This incident, reported in the
newspapers, occurred in California; some men uncovered the
remains of thousands of bodies (and body parts) in a shipping
container. This tragic event was detailed in a book published
in the 1980s entitled *The Woodland Hills Tragedy*.

As a final example, a Baptist minister uncovered firm evidence
of human bodies in a city dumpster in Odessa, Texas. Olga Fairfax reported:

> In Odessa, Texas, city ordinance 69-91 forbids placing a
> dead animal in a dumpster. But that didn't stop one abor-
> tionist from depositing large brown plastic bags full of
> sock-like gauze bags into the city dumpster prior to closing
> every night.[49]

A Baptist minister opened the bags and to his horror found
little "perfectly formed hands and feet of a 13-week-old baby
and the complete body, in pieces, of a 17-week-old baby. Everything except one foot was there: The rib cage, sexual organs,
head, fingernails and toe nails."[50]

1.7 Commercial Use of the Fetus

Companies, especially some pharmaceutical and cosmetic-
related industries, have been using collagen, a jelly-like sub-
stance found in tissue, bone and cartilage. Collagen may also
come from the placenta; however, except for animal collagen or
bovine collagen products, collagen-enriched products (for example, cosmetics, shampoos) may contain human collagen from
fetuses.

In addition to collagen, other human tissue from the fetus is
sometimes used by the cosmetic industry. For instance, the trade
in fetal tissue, as of 1984, was at least one million dollars annu-

ally for hysterotomy-aborted (late-term) fetuses. Other commercial uses of fetuses have included the encasement of human embryos and organs in plastic and their sale as novelty paperweights. In addition, Olga Fairfax reported that, in Great Britain, soap (reminiscent of Nazi Germany) has been made from aborted babies' fat.[51]

Plentiful details exist in regard to the commercial use of the fetus. The fetal items sold (or processed and then sold) demonstrate that the vendors regard the fetus as human. A French company's catalog advertised a "Whole Human Embryo" and various whole fetal organs.[52] The *Chicago Sun-Times* reported that an American medical research company was testing the hearts, brains, and other organs from 100 fetuses as part of a $350,000 pesticide research contract. According to one person, there was even "some dispute" over whether the fetuses were living or dead.[53]

Journalist Suzanne Rini pointed out in her book *Beyond Abortion: A Chronicle of Fetal Experimentation* that the *Cork* (Ireland) *Examiner* reported experimentation with human fetuses by the cosmetics industry. The newspaper article stated:

> Laboratories in Europe, which serve the cosmetic industry in the preparation of beauty products, are experimenting on live human fetuses. This horrific claim is made in an as yet unpublished report to a Committee of the European Parliament...In his report [to the European Parliament, Italian Christian Democrat Member of Parliament, Alberto Ghergo] says that in (unnamed) European embryological laboratories experiments are being carried out on fetuses between 12 and 21 weeks. These are removed whole and alive by means of hysterotomy (Caesarean Section)...The embryos are dissected in order to remove certain organs (pancreas, thymus, brain, etc.) which are frozen by liquid nitrogen vapours. Other embryos are frozen on extraction from the mother's womb to be set aside for various uses.[54]

The presence of the pancreas, thymus and brain (removed from the fetus) is worth noting as we examine the humanity of the fetus.

There is evidence that some fetuses are aborted alive, allowed to die without medical assistance, and then harvested for organs and tissues.[55]

There are many more examples of the commercial use of the fetus. One company listed fetuses (as "embryos"), which were three months of age, in one of their customer catalogs. The catalog described the fetuses as "bisected along the median, cleared and mounted naturally." The catalog stated, under the same ad, "Specify age or ages desired."[56]

Actual preserved fetuses (often obtained through abortion) seem quite popular in the commercial world. Regardless of their popularity, these models provide additional evidence of the results of abortion and bear on the humanity of the fetus. A company in Cannes, France, advertised:

> Beauty by Freezing: A revolutionary treatment of cellular regeneration uses freezing. Since the work of Dr. Alexis Carrel, we know that young cells applied to old tissues are able to regenerate them. These cells are the more effective if they are living.[57]

The same leaflet advertised: "Red bottle contains placenta, spleen, liver and thymus of the fetus."[58]

In summary, the commercial use of the fetus involves body parts harvested for commercial use. All of the material harvested (for example, placenta, skin, collagen, fat) is valued precisely because it is human.

1.8 Scientific Use of the Fetus

An additional area for our study is the scientific use of the fetus. Some researchers' rationale for performing research on human fetuses is that the fetuses are human, not animal. The fetus has body parts (for example, lungs, liver) ideal for scientific research and experimentation. The following cases reported by Olga Fairfax and by Suzanne Rini involved use of human fetuses:

"A rabies vaccine is produced from viruses grown in the lungs of aborted children, according to FDA. A polio vaccine was also grown with cells from aborted kids."[59]

"Brain cells would be 'harvested' from aborted babies for transplant."[60]

Human fetal antigens have been obtained by homogenizing bodies of fetuses, according to a report in the *Journal of the American Medical Association,* March 26, 1973.[61]

"A $600,000 grant from N.I.H. enabled one baby (among many others in the experiment done in Finland) to be sliced open without an anesthetic so that a liver could be obtained. The researcher in charge said that the baby was complete and was even 'secreting urine.' He disclaimed the need for anesthetic, saying an aborted baby is just garbage."[62]

"A study on the severed heads of 12 babies delivered by C section who were kept alive for months"[63] was also reported.

The cases above are only several of many incidents of the scientific use of an aborted fetus, dead or alive. Scientific use of the fetus can be divided into several categories, two of which will be reviewed here: federally funded fetal research and the use of live aborted fetuses.

The *Roe v. Wade* decision, which opened the door to abortion on demand in 1973, eventually ushered in the scientific use of dead (and living) fetuses for experimentation. The fetuses ranged from healthy late-term babies (harvested, as the fetus was meant to be aborted) to early tissues and organs from suction abortions. A special category included the unhealthy fetuses, those with defects.[64] Many fetuses with defects have been rejected by their parents, aborted because of a defect, and used for experimentation.

1.8A Federally Funded Fetal Research

A preface is necessary in order to document the federally funded research involving dead (and, sometimes, living) fetuses often obtained from abortion. The development of the "tissue" school of thought (that is, that fetuses are mere tissue and not living humans), along with the argument that aborting a fetus can save or enhance the lives of wanted fetuses, became the premise for fetal research, including grants for abortions and experimentation on living fetuses. The fetal experiments presented below indicate that many "scientists" are busy harvesting organs (many from fetuses obtained by induced abortions) for biomedical knowledge and scientific advancement without considering whether the fetus has any rights.

NIH-Funded Research

The National Institutes of Health (NIH) have been a primary source of federal funding of fetal research. The details of these experiments show a scientific use of body parts and organs, all taken from the fetus. The following is a list of some of the NIH-funded research on the fetus:

"Normal and Abnormal Utero-Vaginal Development" was studied using reproductive tracts of aborted fetuses. Gerald R. Cunha of the University of California, San Francisco, was given $229,382 to perform this work in 1984-1985.[65]

For "24-hour collection of fresh abortuses," Dr. Thomas Shephard of the University of Seattle was given $100,975 in 1984-1985.[66]

Fetal skin specimens were used by Dr. Karen Holbrook of the University of Washington, Seattle, in her study of "Fetal Skin Biology." For her work she was granted $239,740 in 1984-85. The specimens included as many as "sixty human embryos...obtained by hysterectomy, hysterotomy, or saline suction abortion."[67]

The above samples represent only a portion of the federally assisted fetal research within the past two decades. A detailed look at the specifics of these cases gives us insight into human characteristics of the fetus.

Dr. Cunha reported that he used "completely non-viable"

aborted specimens' reproductive tracts. These came, he said, from first-trimester dilation-and-curettage abortions or from second-trimester dilation and evacuation; in both methods, the fetus is shredded. He then took hairless mice and transplanted some of the fetal reproductive tract into the mouse.[68] Certainly a "fetal reproductive tract" is a human characteristic. Other cases also reveal biologically human parts.

Dr. Holbrook's specimens were, as mentioned, 60 human embryos from abortions. Her experiments can further be described as follows: For use in her work with fetal skin, she received fetal skin biopsies from two sources. The first was normal abortuses of the first, second and third trimesters. "When asked about their state of abortion, she said, 'Hopefully they are not born alive. It's better to avoid that. The skin is taken after fetal demise.' "[69]

Obviously, "skin...taken after fetal demise" denotes a body part taken after a death. In fact, the irony of many pro-abortion arguments is that a fetus is not considered a human being during the abortion, but when wanted for experimentation, it is supplied to scientists for *human* organs and body parts. Even the researchers themselves admit that the fetus enables science to experiment with *human* models. Perhaps the following statement from Dr. Cunha best illustrates this:

"There are animal models for studying everything we do. It's likely we won't learn anything new [by working on animals]. [But] when you get a positive result in a human, you can be sure."[70]

1.8B Use of Live Aborted Fetuses

The following cases reported by journalist Suzanne Rini describe the use of living fetal bodies in medical experimentation:

In a test to develop an artificial placenta, a doctor practiced and tested equipment on "living, aborted babies whom, above all, he could not allow to survive" the experiment. In essence, he "willfully gave experimental therapeutic help to an aborted baby of seven months' gestation, but, in the end, did not allow the baby to survive."[71]

"A *Cambridge* [England] *Evening News* report stated that 'a storm of protest blew up in England when a Member of Parliament learned that private abortion clinics had been selling live babies for research.' " Said one doctor, "We are simply using something which is destined for the incinerator to benefit mankind..."[72]

A moving, excreting fetus, obtained from a hysterotomy abortion, was used by a doctor for organ harvest at Yale-New Haven Hospital. The medical student who assisted at the operation on the live fetus got "sort of pale" and "sick in his stomach" shortly after the operation.[73]

According to one observer, Pittsburgh's Magee Women's Hospital "packed aborted babies in ice while still moving and shipped them to experimental labs."[74]

Ms. Wester Anderson quoted a report published in the *Washington Post* on April 15, 1973,which stated that a Dr. Gaull had injected "radioactive chemicals into umbilical cords of fetuses." While the heart was still beating, he removed their brains, lungs, liver, and kidneys for study.[75]

The cases above represent only a few of the examples of scientific experimentation on live fetuses. It is important to note that the development of prostaglandin, an abortifacient drug used in late abortions that results in the delivery of a whole, sometimes live, baby has further increased experimentation on whole, living fetuses.

2

Medical Evidence

The photographs within this chapter show the results of abortion, that is, three fetuses that were legally aborted within the United States. Although by scientific definition the unborn is called a fetus at approximately the 12th week of pregnancy (prior to that it is classed as an embryo), human development is a continuum. The photographs depict fetuses of 6.5, 19, and 24.5 weeks gestation.

All human organs are present within a fetus by eight to ten weeks' gestation. The youngest fetus shown, while not yet having all organs, has key organs, such as a male reproductive organ, and the genetic makeup which is specifically human. The other fetuses have detailed human characteristics (for example, hair, nose and eyebrows).

There are seven primary types of abortion procedures. (A new procedure, performed with the drug RU-486, has been developed recently but is not discussed here. The drug was not legal in the United States as of 1992.) The seven procedures are detailed below. Studio photographs of the three fetuses are presented on the pages following.

D and C (dilation-and-curettage) abortion uses a loop-tipped knife to cut the fetus into pieces before it is removed from the womb. This method is used on fetuses of seven to 12 weeks (or more) gestation.

Dilation-and-evacuation abortion uses forceps with teeth. This method is similar to dilation-and-curettage; as this method is used on older fetuses (of 12 to 20 or more weeks gestation) the fetus' head must be crushed and the body torn apart in order to remove the pieces from the womb.

Hysterotomy abortion is similar to Caesarean section both in that the fetus is removed through an abdominal incision and in that a live baby is the usual result. The fetus is put into a bucket, where it is left to die. This method is used on fetuses of eight to 19 weeks gestation.

Prostaglandin abortion uses an injection of the drug prostaglandin to induce premature labor. This method is used on fetuses of 12 to 20 or more weeks gestation, and is commonly used for abortions in the seventh, eighth and ninth months of pregnancy. If the result of the prostaglandin abortion is a live baby (and it frequently is), the baby is almost always left to die.

Salt-poisoning abortion uses an injection of concentrated saline solution to poison and burn the fetus, which is then expelled by miscarriage. This method is used on fetuses of 14 or more weeks gestation.

Suction-curettage abortion uses a suction machine to dismember the fetus in the womb and suck the pieces into a jar. This method is used on fetuses of 13 or fewer weeks gestation.

D & X (Dilation-and-Extraction) abortion uses a suction catheter to draw the brains from a living fetus whose head is still within the womb (the rest of the body having already been removed) during the late second and even early third trimester. This enables the skull to be collapsed for easy removal of the rest of the fetus from the mother's body, and it ensures that the fetus will not accidentally be born alive. The fetal brain tissue can then be used for experimentation.

Stephen (named by the curators of the fetus) was of approximately 6.5 weeks gestation, two inches long, weighing one to three ounces. Stephen's body is immersed in a formaldehyde solution for preservation. The fetus at this stage is developed in the sense that most of the organs are present. The limbs are noticeable; tiny male genitals are identifiable near the umbilical cord.

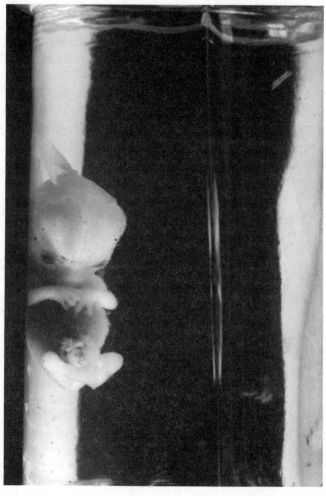

Photograph by Scott Cross; courtesy of Sanctity of Life, Annandale, VA.

Esther was of approximately 19 weeks gestation, 14 inches long, weighing ten ounces (283 grams). Esther was aborted by the injection of a highly concentrated salt solution, which burned her outer layer of skin and poisoned her. The photograph shows hair and fingernails. The dark spots are burned skin. The fetus at this stage is fully developed with all the organs present.

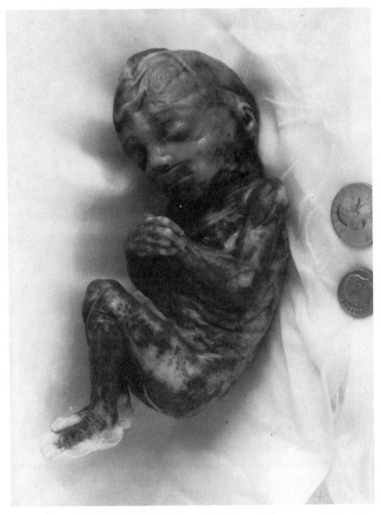

Photograph by Scott Cross; courtesy of Sanctity of Life, Annandale, VA.

Grace was of approximately 24.5 weeks gestation, 19 inches long, weighing one pound, 2.3 ounces (519 grams). Grace was aborted by the drug prostaglandin. From the photograph, there is evidence of hair and fingernails. The photo also verifies that the fetus at this stage is fully developed in the sense that all of the organs are present.

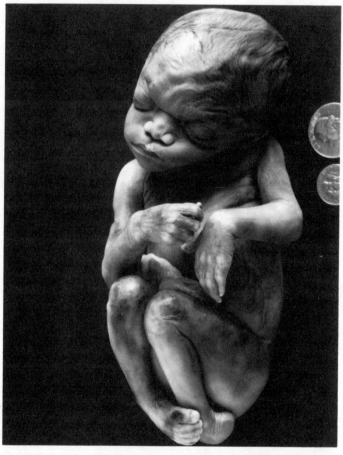

Photograph by Scott Cross; courtesy of Sanctity of Life, Annandale, VA.

3

Emotional Evidence

(Note: The following question and answer are from the author's September, 1990 interview with Pamela Carr, who had an abortion.)

Q: *"Did you have any feeling that a human life was being destroyed? If so, explain."*

A: "I remember being asked to sign a form stating that the abortion facility had the right to discard of any fetal tissue and/or matter. I remember asking myself why this form was necessary. After being led into an operating room and putting two and two together about the other signs that I saw, the veil of ignorance was lifted. I knew that I had killed my baby."

Women who have had abortions, their associated spouses or "lovers," as well as medical personnel examined in studies reveal a sense of human loss and other negative emotions relative to abortion. Suicidal emotions are also sometimes experienced after an abortion.

The information below documents the emotions pertaining to the abortion of the fetus. This includes psychological evidence before, during, and especially after an abortion. A personal interview is also included.

The following sections are presented within this chapter:

Abortion Trauma
Women and Abortion

The Effect of Abortion on "Would-Have-Been Fathers":
   Post-Traumatic Stress Disorder
Statements from Medical Personnel
Emotional Evidence: A Personal Testimony

3.1 Abortion Trauma

Abortion trauma can be defined as the typical emotions following an abortion. The term "abortion trauma" includes, but is not limited to, the following:

Depression
Regret
Sadness
Sense of guilt
Sense of loss
Horror (experienced during nightmares and/or flashbacks).

3.2 Women and Abortion

Recent magazine and newspaper accounts reveal women's emotional and psychological conditions following an abortion. These accounts, while varied, were taken from among the many women who have expressed negative emotions about their decision to abort. These emotions include severe depression, feelings of guilt, regret, sadness, sense of loss, etc.

While some women's accounts indicate that they have no symptoms of abortion trauma, many studies conclude that women often suppress or repress painful emotions following an abortion. For instance, a Canadian study verified that women who denied any post-abortion remorse during polling were often suppressing or repressing deep emotional/psychological after-effects.

The following quotation from Willke's *Abortion...Questions and Answers* discusses this study:

> **Q:** *But most polls show few emotional problems—only a sense of relief!*

A: Yes, but "What women really feel at the deepest level about abortion is very different from what they say in reply to questionnaires." A Canadian study took a group of women, questioned them, and then subjected a randomly chosen one-half of the study group to in-depth psychotherapy, even though they denied problems.[1]

The results of the Canadian study included the following:

"What emerged from psychotherapy was in sharp contrast [to the questionnaires], even when the woman had rationally considered abortion to be inevitable, the only course of action." It was demonstrated that the conscious, rationalized decision for an abortion can coexist with profound rejection of it at the deepest level.[2]

The same article continued: "Despite surface appearances, abortion leaves behind deeper feelings, 'invariably of intense pain, involving bereavement and a sense of identification with the fetus.' "[3]

Below are a few examples of the many cases involving common emotional/psychological symptoms reported by women following an abortion:

Depression

Women suffer depression, sometimes to a suicidal degree, after an abortion. Thousands of such cases have been documented, including the following accounts. One woman stated:

It was difficult when I began to become depressed. The abortion issue began to surface in my mind, the acknowledgment of it. It had been repressed for a very long time. My husband never knew that I had had an abortion. It was not something that I had ever told anyone. It was just part of my past. There came a point in time when I finally had to tell him because I had become a basically very nonfunctional human being. I was doing nothing except sitting in a chair staring at a wall all day long, thinking about how I could kill myself.[4]

Another woman revealed:

> I quit school at that time. I tried to commit suicide at that
> time. I couldn't carry on any relationships at that time—not
> with my family, boyfriends, friends. Everything fell apart
> because of that.[5]

A third instance demonstrates a similar severe case of
depression:

> I was on the faculty of this reputable university and still
> couldn't get rid of this self-hatred. And so I decided to
> kill myself—once my family rejected me.[6]

One report even stated that two teenage mothers, following
their abortions, "attempted suicide on the very dates their babies
would have been born."[7]

As a final example of the myriad of women who experience
severe, often suicidal, depression following an abortion, there
is the following woman's recollection of her post-abortion emotional state:

> By the end of my fifth semester at college, I was flunking
> every class. I had become heavily involved in drugs and
> alcohol and was often suicidal. I hated myself and had no
> ambition or desire to live.[8]

Scientific research also shows that a woman who has had an
abortion is more prone to depression during a subsequent pregnancy. Willke described another study:

> It is interesting that early in the next pregnancy, "Eight
> of 21 women who had obtained a past abortion were found
> to be clinically depressed and anxious. In contrast, only
> 8 of 98 who had not had abortions were depressed."[9]

Regret, Sadness

Other symptoms, often experienced by women who have had
abortions, are regret and sadness.

> After my abortion, I immediately woke up in regret and
> in grief and I recall screaming, and I couldn't stand it. I
> had to get out of there.[10]

Another woman stated:

> Feeling my baby being torn from my womb was one of the worst sensations I've ever experienced. As the machine tried to suck out my insides, everything was trying to move up in my body to escape being pulled out. The vibration made me feel extremely nauseated.
>
> I wasn't sure how much of this I could take. The counselor must have sensed my panic because she reassured me it was almost over. I grabbed her hand and squeezed it tightly until the machine went off...
>
> Coming out of that clinic, I felt as if I had just lived through a nightmare. I felt humiliated, patronized, ashamed, cheap, degraded, and ruined—the whole spectrum of the most negative feelings a woman could ever experience. I felt so sick that I didn't even feel relieved.[11]

A Sense of Guilt

A sense of guilt is another painful emotion that women frequently experience after an abortion. One woman's account follows:

> The pain which I had been trying very poorly to cope with for three, four months after this abortion, the self-hatred and tremendous guilt that had built in me which I could not in any way get rid of...[12]

Medical studies also confirm that a sense of guilt often appears after an abortion. For example, the *American Journal of Psychiatry* stated that "patients clearly functioned well before the abortion and later experienced psychoses precipitated by guilt over the abortion."[13]

Sense of Loss, Flashbacks, Nightmares and Other Negative Emotions

Emotions experienced by a woman following an abortion often involve a sense of loss, which includes flashbacks, nightmares, etc. In her book *Choices,* discussing "The Complications of Abortion," Judie Brown states:

A study by Dr. Anne Speckhard of the University of Minnesota found that more than half of the women who have had abortions suffer from nightmares and flashbacks related to their abortion experiences. Nearly one in four experienced hallucinations; thirty-five percent believed their dead baby returned to visit them in dreams or visions. [14]

A careful analysis of other psychological studies on this subject provides additional evidence of post-abortion stress disorder.

3.3 The Effect of Abortion on "Would-Have-Been Fathers": Post-Traumatic Stress Disorder

What about the man who would have been the father of a baby if an abortion had not taken place? Research indicates that a man, especially when he realizes that his offspring was aborted, also experiences severe negative emotions.

For various reasons, the man involved in the conception of the fetus sometimes never knows about the abortion. This is primarily because of the woman's desire to keep the abortion extremely confidential. Consequently, there are fewer accounts of men's reactions to the abortion of their offspring. Below is a typical account of the traumatic effect of abortion on men who are aware that their offspring was aborted. Most importantly, the following account provides further emotional evidence of the humanity of the fetus.

> You've probably read about what unresolved guilt and repressed emotions have done to the Vietnam vet. They call it "Post Traumatic Stress Disorder." It is basically the result of trying to erase or suppress the intense reaction to the death and violence that surrounded them. This is the same type reaction I had to my wife's abortion. For me it wasn't over when we walked out of that clinic after the abortion. [15]

This former father-to-be, who consented to his wife's decision to abort their most recent offspring at that time, described his initial experience of entering the clinic as similar to that of his emotional upheaval in the Vietnam War. He said:

> I'll never forget what it was like walking down into that waiting room . . .
>
> I had to leave because of the vibes I felt. . . I had first-hand knowledge of what I'd felt in that place. I had been a soldier during the last of Vietnam (1970-1973) and worked on rescue squads after my separation from the Army. What I felt in the abortion clinic was the air of death. The hopelessness and despair hung in the waiting room like a fog. I couldn't stand to be in there. I didn't want my wife in there, either.[16]

The husband and his wife left the clinic without having the abortion; however, they had "decided to see a doctor who did abortions at his office." At first, the "friendly" and "personable" atmosphere at the doctor's office seemed great. The abortion went "without a hitch, and that afternoon my wife and I spent together was one of the closest times of our marriage. It was all over, or so we thought."[17]

Like many of the people who have consented to abortions, this man "suppressed" or "buried" his feelings. He stated: "But since visiting that first abortion clinic, I knew deep inside that what we were planning was not right. I really did not feel at peace with our decision."[18]

As with many post-abortion men and women, the lingering emotional effects of abortion destroyed this couple's marriage. A deep bitterness and anger developed. The husband described it as follows:

> Throughout the course of that time the feeling of guilt gnawed away at me, until I had to do what I learned so well in the Army; I hardened my heart and buried my feelings. But I couldn't keep the lid on them all the time. Just as the buried pain and resentment from my military duty would at times explode like a volcano, so would the bitterness about losing the child.[19]

The couple separated one year after the abortion and divorced a few months after that. The abortion, while not the only reason for their divorce, contributed to the breakup.[20]

In concluding his account, the man stated:

> When my wife and I were facing this [decision regarding abortion], we were not getting the facts from the health clinic or the abortion clinic. No one told us that there were long-term effects from abortion. No one told us that many people involved with abortions suffer guilt, depression, and regret long after the abortion itself.[21]

The same man said he came to believe that abortion is one of life's "decisions that will have far-reaching consequences."[22]

3.4 Statements From Medical Personnel

Negative emotions (for example, sorrow, sense of loss of life) are also evident in statements from medical personnel involved in abortion. This information adds further strength to the emotional evidence.

For example, consider one nurse's candid recognition of the abortion procedure:

> We do abortions here; that is all we do. There are weary, grim moments when I think I cannot bear another basin of bloody remains, utter another kind phrase of reassurance. So I leave the procedure room in the back and reach for a new chart...
>
> I prepare myself for another basin, another brief and chafing loss.[23]

The nurse also admitted, "I watch a woman's swollen abdomen sink to softness in a few stuttering moments and my own belly flip-flops with sorrow."[24] In addition, she stated: "But a well of woe seems to open beneath many women when they hear that thumping sound."[25]

Another article showed that medical personnel know that the fetus is not simply a "blob." The article, concerning a doctor who performed abortions, stated:

> After an abortion, the doctor must inspect these remains
> to make sure that all the fetal parts and the placenta have
> been removed. Any tissue left inside the uterus can start
> an infection. Dr. Bours squeezed the contents of the sock
> into a shallow dish and poked about with a finger. "You
> can see a teeny-tiny hand," he said.[26]

Another worker in the same office stated: "We all wish it were
formless, but it's not...And it's painful. There's a lot of emotional pain."[27]

The above statements verify the sense of human loss during
an abortion. Medical personnel often describe subsequent feelings of sadness and other negative emotions.

Magda Denes, a physician, argued in her own published
research that abortion is both a sorrow and a necessity: a necessity, she argued, because women need them, and a sorrow
because a human life is taken.[28]

Another doctor, after viewing a well-known ultrasound film,
The Silent Scream (a documentary of the abortion procedure),
became very "nauseated." This doctor had been a colleague of
the film's producer, Dr. Nathanson. However, while Dr. Nathanson had stopped doing abortions, this doctor had continued to
perform them—until he saw *The Silent Scream.* The emotional
effect of the film on this doctor was described by journalist Jim
Edwards:

> One viewing of the footage was enough. Like the ultra-
> sound technician, the doctor who had performed the abor-
> tion became so nauseated by what he had witnessed on
> the screen that he was forced to turn away in order to com-
> pose himself. He has never performed another abortion.[29]

Consider also the following statements from the *American
Journal of Obstetrics and Gynecology* and *Family Planning Perspective,* respectively:

Nurses were more disturbed by amniocentesis abortions (salt poisoning and Prostaglandin) in which they played major roles in supporting the patient as well in her abortion.[30]

Reconstruction of the fetal sections after removal is necessary to ensure completeness of the abortion procedure. Clearly, D & E transfers much of the possible psychological trauma of the abortion from the patient to the professional.[31]

Lastly, an *Ob/Gyn News* article of 1978 presented a frank admission by an abortionist:

...the emotional turmoil that the procedure inevitably wreaks on physicians and staff....There is no possibility of denial of an act of destruction by the operator....The sensations of dismemberment flow through the forceps like an electric current....[32]

3.5 Emotional Evidence: A Personal Testimony—The following is an abortion in retrospect: the author's interview with Pamela Carr in September of 1990. Ms. Carr recounted her emotions before, during and after an abortion. Ms. Carr has been active with Black Americans for Life and American Victims of Abortion, as well as other organizations.

Emotional/Psychological Questionnaire on Abortion

Before

1. *"What initial specific thoughts and emotions did you experience when pondering your possible abortion?"*

"My initial thought in regards to having an abortion was at first denial of my pregnancy. I never actually believed I would have an abortion because I was in a state of shock. I couldn't believe that I was pregnant."

2. *"Would you summarize your emotions, prior to the abortion, as more negative (e.g., sadness) than positive (e.g., happiness), or vice versa?"*

"Prior to my abortion I had mixed feelings. I was sad because I was pregnant and felt as if my entire life would be ruined if I had to become a mother. My sadness subsided when I began to deny the fact that I was having a baby and it was growing inside of me. Reducing my child to a blob of tissue made me feel better about what I was going to do."

3. *"Did you feel emotionally or psychologically pressured to obtain an abortion?"*

"Yes, I did feel pressured to obtain an abortion. I didn't feel that I had any other choice, mostly because I didn't want my family and friends to find out. Abortion was an acceptable choice and my only option back then."

4. *"Did you feel emotionally and/or psychologically uneasy about the possibility of an abortion? If so, describe."*

"I felt extremely uneasy. I kept struggling with the idea that I was taking a life. I refused to allow myself to believe that this could be so. I tried to rationalize that it was only a blob of tissue and not a baby."

5. *"Prior to the actual day of the abortion, did you feel reminded or preoccupied about life in your womb?"*

"I was very preoccupied. I wanted to know for certain if I was carrying a baby. It seemed during that time that my curiosity could not be satisfied. I felt tormented by what I was sensing. I remember the night before not being able to sleep because my decision made me feel so uneasy."

During

1. *"Summarize your true emotions/psychological state during the abortion."*

"During the abortion I was heavily sedated and unaware of what was going on. A few moments before, I was terribly fearful.

I remember the doctor telling me not to be afraid or nervous as he saw the expression of terror on my face. I was terrified!"

2. *"Did you cry during the abortion? Why?"*

"I didn't cry during the abortion, because I was asleep. I did feel extremely depressed, though, when I woke up because I knew I had taken the life of my baby. I hated what I had done but there was nothing I could do to bring back my child. I was so depressed. I cried. The guilt I felt was unbearable."

3. *"Did you have any feeling that a human life was being destroyed? If so, explain."*

"I remember being asked to sign a form stating that the abortion facility had the right to discard of any fetal tissue and or matter. I remember asking myself why this form was necessary. After being led into an operating room and putting two and two together about the other signs I saw, the veil of ignorance was lifted. I knew that I had killed my baby."

After

1. *"As recently as 1989, major news magazines have reported on several women's feelings/emotions following their abortions. Although some of the women claim to hold no guilt or remorse (or other negative emotions) about the choice to abort, many studies indicate that women often suppress or repress negative emotions about a previous abortion. With this realization in mind, did you experience any of the emotions listed below (which many women claim to experience even years later)? If so, using an arbitrary scale of 1 to 10 (10 being the most intense), rank and comment on your response relative to the list below. Scale: 1=lowest intensity; 10=highest intensity."*

a. Guilt: "Scale 10. Before, during, and after I struggled with guilt."

b. Regret: "Scale 10. Directly after, I regretted my actions."

c. Sadness: "Scale 10. I had problems going on with my life as usual. I had problems with school and even failed a class."

d. Sense of loss: "Scale 10. I instantly began to think about when my child would have been born."

e. Anxiety: "Scale 8. I couldn't rest because of what I had done. I was always trying to find something to ease the pain."

f. Depression: "Scale 10. I had bouts of depression after, for at least four years."

Before, During and After

1. *"Reflecting on your abortion decision, do you recall attempting to suppress or repress negative emotions (e.g., sadness, guilt, remorse) at any time before, during, or after the abortion? If so, describe."*

"I repressed negative emotions to deal mostly with the loss of my child. Directly after the abortion, I refused to think about the fact that I had murdered my child."

Conclusion

The information in this chapter verifies that negative (and often severely negative) emotions exist on the part of men and women involved in the abortion procedure. These emotions suggest that the fetus is more than a mere object; indeed, the aborted fetus is often the cause of emotional trauma.

4

Legal Evidence

By Robert B. French

> And let the legislator and the moralist look to it;
> for as sure as there is in any nation a hidden tamper-
> ing with infant life, whether frequent or occasional,
> systematic or accidental, so sure will the chastisement
> of the Almighty fall on such a nation.[1]
>
> —Augustus B. Granville in *Sudden Death*

On January 22, 1973, in *Roe v. Wade,* the U.S. Supreme Court opened the door to abortion on demand by declaring a Texas law against abortion unconstitutional. As a result, abortion has become the most common surgical procedure in America. Thus, it may seem foolish to turn to the law for evidence concerning the humanity of the fetus—and certainly that would be the case if we looked only at *Roe v. Wade.* However, *Roe v. Wade* is so unlike other abortion laws and court decisions that it would be very unwise to use it as a guideline for our purposes.

All previous U.S. abortion laws and rulings, for example, recognized penalties for abortion, the assumption being that there is something—or someone—in the womb worthy of protection. *Roe v. Wade,* almost overnight, set up very broad conditions under which abortion would be allowed, while completely ignoring the question of the fetus' humanity. Justice Blackmun stated bluntly in his opening argument, "The Court need not address the difficult question of when life begins."[2]

This statement alone should arouse our suspicion and moral outrage—but further on, *Roe v. Wade* takes an even more sinister turn, setting up its own arbitrary timetable to determine when a fetus may be "terminated," and under what conditions.

Blackmun, acknowledging the "State's important and legitimate interest in potential life," states that "the compelling point is at viability. This is so because the fetus then presumably has the capability of meaningful life outside the mother's womb."[3] Thus, *Roe* opened the door to abortion on demand without defining the exact point at which a new human life is present in the womb.

Decades later, neither the legislative branch nor the Supreme Court of the U.S. government has acted on the evidence that a unique human life begins at conception. Moreover, the court has yet even to *affirm* what scientific evidence confirms: an identifiable human exists within the womb early in the first trimester—and this in spite of more recent decisions such as *Webster v. Reproductive Health Services,* which allowed states to pass certain restrictions on abortion (e.g., requiring a viability test on the fetus).[4] The focus of abortion law may even soon shift from the question: "Under what circumstances will the law allow a life to be ended?" to "Under what circumstances will the law allow a life to be brought into this world?"

Roe v. Wade helped create the social attitude that the fetus may not be human. However, a thorough study of legal evidence, both past and present, supports the humanity of the fetus and its right to legal protection. The following legal concepts will be examined below:

Historical Laws to Protect the Fetus (English common laws against abortion and American law before *Roe v. Wade*)

The Thoughts of the Framers of the Constitution and Constitutional Protection of Human Life

The Capability of the Fetus to Survive Outside the Womb

Recent Laws Restricting Abortion

Justices Recognizing the Humanity of the Unborn

The Ban on Federal Abortion Funding

The Rule Against Perpetuities (an inheritance/estate law).

4.1 Historical Laws to Protect the Fetus

4.1A English Common Laws Against Abortion

Common laws in England against abortion were used as the foundation for American law. Before modern medicine was able to show that life begins at conception, laws existed to protect the fetus. In the United States, the earliest laws against abortion stemmed from English Common Law. Henry of Bracton, who virtually founded common law with the writing of his book, *The Laws and Customs of England,* stated:

> If one strikes a pregnant woman or gives her poison in order to procure an abortion, if the foetus is already formed or quickened, especially if it is quickened, he commits homicide.[5]

Bracton's statement, like the statements below, was generally based on what science knew at that time: the fetus was a living human being when the mother felt its movement (quickening). Since Bracton's time, technology has enabled science to photograph a tiny human "swimming" in its mother's womb well before "quickening."

Sir William Blackstone, whom many consider to have had the greatest influence on early American law, characterized "life" as "the immediate gift of God, a right inherent by nature in every individual; and it begins in contemplation of law as soon as an infant is able to stir in the mother's womb."[6] Blackstone also referenced and admired previous law stating that if a woman were "quick with child" and the child was born dead due to a beating or "potion" (administering of an abortifacient), the crime was manslaughter. However, if the child was born alive and subsequently died due to the potion or beating, the crime was murder.[7] Quickening was generally thought to be the period from "the one hundred and fifteenth to the one hundred and thirtieth day after conception...."[8]

English statutory law went further than English Common Law that named abortion a crime by enacting the Ellenborough Act of 1803. This law extended the crime to the period *before* quickening, and was specifically aimed at the use of abortifacients or instrumental or mechanical violence upon the fetus. If the child died before quickening, the defendant was "liable to be fined, imprisoned, set in and upon the pillory. . .or to be transported beyond the seas for any Term not exceeding fourteen years." Death was the penalty for abortions performed after quickening.[9] The law was modified again by Lord Lansdowne to include penalties for instrumental or mechanical violence after quickening, and death was still the penalty for performing an abortion after quickening.[10] A subsequent English law removed the death penalty. It is interesting to note that English law showed the belief—Dr. Horatio R. Storer, a physician and member of the American Medical Association (AMA) called it a "mistaken belief"—in a "difference of guilt" according to whether the abortion took place before or after quickening.[11] Echoes of this belief are heard today in the debate over viability, the point at which a child is capable of sustaining independent life outside the womb.

4.1B American Law Before Roe v. Wade

In the original thirteen colonies, abortion was a crime under common law if movements of the fetus were "perceptible"; and this law remained when the Constitution was adopted.[12] John T. Noonan, in his book *A Private Choice,* reminds us, "What the framers knew to be a crime at common law in the states when they made the Constitution, they did not intend to legalize; indeed, the protection afforded the unborn at common law accorded with their view of the protection to be afforded persons."[13]

The following samples of America's earliest pro-life laws clearly show their link to the English common law and to those who held that life in the womb is sacred:

A 1716 New York City law forbade midwives to "Give any Counsel or Administer any Herb, Medicine or Potion, or any other thing to any Woman being with Child whereby She Should Destroy or Miscarry that she goeth withall before her time."[14]

A nineteenth-century Connecticut statute, which forbade abortion after quickening, stated:

> Every person who shall willfully and maliciously administer to, or cause to be administered to, or taken by, any woman then being quick with child, any medicine, drug, noxious substance, or other thing, [with] intent thereby to produce the miscarriage of such woman, or to destroy the child of which she is pregnant, or shall willfully and maliciously use and employ any instrument or other means to produce such miscarriage, or to destroy such child, shall suffer imprisonment in the Connecticut State prison for a term not less than seven nor more than ten years.[15]

A Virginia statute in 1849, which outlawed abortion throughout pregnancy but required proof of pregnancy, stated:

> Any free person who shall administer to, or cause to be taken, by a woman, any drug or other thing, or use any means, with intent to destroy her unborn child, or to produce abortion or miscarriage, and shall thereby destroy such child, or produce such abortion or miscarriage, shall be confined in the penitentiary not less than one, nor more than five years. No person, by reason of any act mentioned in this section, shall be punishable where such act is done in good faith, with the intention of saving the life of such woman or child.[16]

Despite the laws that existed, many persons were not satisfied. Dr. Horatio R. Storer led a crusade in the 1880s to toughen the abortion laws. Storer's main concern was the "unscientific distinction between the status of the unborn before and after quickening," and he noted how this distinction "permitted abortion in early pregnancy."[17] In his book *On Criminal Abortion in America,* Storer observed that quickening "is often absent, even throughout pregnancy," and "is therefore as unlikely a period for the commencement of foetal life as those others set by Hippocrates and his successors, varying from the third day after conception, to that of the Stoics, namely birth, and as false as them all."[18] Storer examined the statutes of his time, most of them based on common law, and concluded that they did not offer enough protection to the unborn. He stated that most laws required proof of pregnancy, usually impossible in those times, or the body of the child, which had often been disposed of secretly or concealed.[19]

The American Medical Association (AMA) crusade helped tighten state laws against abortion. By the end of the nineteenth century, all states protected the life of the fetus from conception through birth.[20] The motivation for the enactment of these laws was the fact, some would say, that life is present from conception and does not begin at some arbitrary stage of pregnancy. The AMA report of 1871 stated the reason very simply: "We had to deal with human life. In a matter of less importance we could entertain no compromise. An honest judge on the bench would call things by their proper names. We could do no less."[21]

These laws remained in force, for the most part, until the 1960's, when pressure for change began. However, many states, when given the chance to liberalize their abortion laws, refused to do so until change was forced on them by *Roe v. Wade*. Although 19 states did change their laws, 31 did not. In these states, change was rejected by referenda (Michigan and North Dakota), by committees, or by legislatures. No state legalized abortion throughout the nine months of pregnancy.[22] This may indicate that the supposed national "mandate" for the liberalization of abortion law, which pro-abortion speakers today make equivalent to the civil rights movement, did not exist in the 1960's and early 1970's.

4.2 The Thoughts of the Framers of the Constitution and Constitutional Protection of Human Life (The Bill of Rights)

The Court held in *Roe v. Wade* that the "right to privacy" supposedly implied in the due process clause of the Fourteenth Amendment extended to a woman's right to "terminate" a pregnancy. (But this so-called "right" to abortion is not an absolute liberty under *Roe v. Wade;* in individual states, abortion can be restricted or prohibited due to the legitimate or compelling interest of the fetus' life.)

The First, Fourth, Fifth and Ninth Amendments also supposedly guarantee this right of privacy. However, the same amendments the Court used to justify abortion via *Roe v. Wade* can more convincingly be used to justify outlawing abortion completely. We can be fairly certain that the authors of these amendments stood by the common law of the time, which made abortion a crime in most instances. The fact that there are no references to abortion in the Constitution does not mean that those living at the time simply accepted abortion as a social fact, any more than they would have accepted drug abuse or child pornography. In all likelihood, the framers omitted direct reference to abortion because social mores generally accepted the fetus as part of the human family.

Both the Fifth and the Fourteenth Amendments provide for the protection of "life." The Fifth Amendment states: "nor shall any person . . . be deprived of life, liberty, or property" by the federal government without "due process of law." The Fourteenth Amendment contains the same protection of life against encroachment by the states. It is not an historical anomaly to speculate on what the congressmen who passed the Fourteenth Amendment thought of abortion, since some of them also approved anti-abortion legislation in Arizona, Colorado, Idaho, Montana and Nevada.[23]

Looking at the congressional debates on the passage of the Fourteenth Amendment, we also find that those who passed this anti-slavery amendment were thinking of posterity, and of the extension of the bill to other helpless minorities besides the slaves. Congressman Jacob Howard said:

> It will, if adopted by the States, forever disable every one of them from passing laws trenching upon these fundamental rights and privileges which pertain to citizens of the United States, and to all persons who may happen to be within their jurisdiction. It establishes equality before the law, and it gives to the humblest, the poorest, the most despised of the race the same rights and the same protection before the law as it gives to the most powerful, the most wealthy, or the most haughty.[24]

The argument that the unborn are not "persons" within the context of the Fourteenth Amendment is the only thread that holds the tenuous logic of *Roe v. Wade* together. But, as one legal scholar has noted, "Few would argue with the proposition that the primary inalienable rights protected by the due process clause of the Fifth and Fourteenth Amendments are human rights. Similarly, the life protected by the clauses is human life."[25]

4.3 The Capability of the Fetus to Survive Outside the Womb

Even *Roe v. Wade* mentions the need to protect unborn human life, at least in the third trimester. For example, Justice Blackmun stated:

> With respect to the State's important and legitimate interest in potential life, the "compelling" point is at viability. This is so because the fetus then presumably has the capability of meaningful life outside the mother's womb.[26]

Taken at face value, this statement is no less than an admission that there is human life inside the womb; if a fetus can survive as a human being outside the womb, it must be human while inside the womb.

It is the concept of viability, and *Roe v. Wade's* arbitrary separation of pregnancy into three trimesters, that has led to the growing discontent with *Roe v. Wade* and the realization that viability cannot be used as the starting point for dealing with life in the womb. In the words of Justice White, who dissented in the Supreme Court's 5-4 decision striking down a Pennsylvania abortion ruling:

> However one answers the metaphysical or theological question whether the fetus is a "human being" or the legal question whether it is a "person," as that term is used in the Constitution, one must at least recognize. . .that there is no nonarbitrary line separating a fetus from a child, or, indeed, an adult human being.[27]

In *Akron v. Akron Center for Reproductive Health,* Justice O'Connor challenged *Roe v. Wade's* own viability as she wrote:

> The Roe framework, then, is clearly on a collision course
> with itself. As the medical risks of various abortion proce-
> dures decrease, the point at which the State may regulate
> for reasons of maternal health is moved further forward
> to actual childbirth. As medical science becomes better
> able to provide for the separate existence of the fetus,
> the point of viability is moved further back toward
> conception.[28]

From a purely legal perspective, then, *Roe v. Wade* is flawed
because it created fixed legal precedent out of something that
was not fixed—the point of viability. Medical technology is
increasing the fetus' capability to survive outside the womb.
Consequently, the current legal definition of viability is being
pushed further back toward conception.

4.4 Recent Laws Restricting Abortion

In 1989, the U.S. Supreme Court case, *Webster v. Reproductive Health Services,* allowed states to determine whether to
impose more restrictions on abortion. As a result, new restrictions on abortion intensified. Between 1989 and 1990 many
attempts were made in various states and territories to restrict
abortion—for example, to require parental notification, or to bar
sex selection as an accepted reason for abortion. Note that sex
selection, a motive for many abortions, refers to the sex of the
fetus (that is, male or female). States that developed restrictions
on abortions in 1989-1990 included Idaho, Louisiana and Pennsylvania. Pennsylvania's restrictions were actually signed into
law in 1990 by the governor of Pennsylvania, and most of them
were upheld by the Supreme Court in the 1992 case entitled
Planned Parenthood v. Casey.

4.5 Justices Recognizing the Humanity of the Unborn

Several cases in the U.S. have upheld the humanity of the
fetus. For instance, a French geneticist, Dr. Jerome Lejeune,
in a case concerning frozen embryos in Tennessee in 1989,

testified against leaving the human embryos, "tiny human beings," in cold storage.[29]

The judge in the same case upheld the frozen embryos as human life. The judge stated:

> Human life begins at conception. Mr. and Mrs. Davis have produced human beings, in vitro, to be known as their child or children.... It serves the best interests of the child, or children, in vitro, for their mother, Mrs. Davis, to be permitted the opportunity to bring them to term through implantation.[30]

If this case applies to embryos, the judge's statement that life begins at conception also applies to the fetus, since the fetus develops from the embryo.

In a New York case, Judge Adrian Burke cited the Declaration of Independence in his dissent from a 1970 New York ruling that permitted abortion on demand for the first six months of pregnancy.[31] "The Declaration," wrote Judge Burke, "has the force of law, and the constitutions of the United States and of the various states must harmonize with its tenets.... It was intended to serve as a perpetual reminder that rulers, legislators, and Judges were without power to deprive human beings of their rights."[32] Burke referred to the "natural law," upon which the Declaration was founded, saying, "The American concept of a natural law binding upon government and citizens alike, to which all positive law must conform, leads back through John Marshall to Edmund Burke and Henry de Bracton and even beyond the Magna Carta to Judean Law."[33]

4.6 The Ban on Federal Abortion Funding

As recently as 1992, program dollars of Title X (Ten), the Public Health Services Act, have been forbidden for use in abortion counseling or abortion procedures within the United States. Title X was established in 1970 to allow the Secretary of Health and Human Services to "make grants to public and private nonprofit entities to establish and operate family planning projects."[34] Part of Title X, Section 1008, contains the following prohibition from 1970: "None of the funds appropriated under this title shall be used in programs where abortion is a method of family planning."[35]

As a recent *Federal Register* document reveals, "This language clearly creates a wall of separation between Title X programs and abortion as a method of family planning."[36] In 1988, the Department of Health and Human Services issued a final rule to enforce the original wording in Title X: no funds under Title X are to be used in programs where abortion is a method of family planning. The federal government uncovered several cases where family-planning clinics indirectly or directly used funds from Title X for abortion, thereby violating Title X. In documentation accompanying the 1988 federal rule to ensure proper use of Title X funds, a woman recounted how some clinics withheld biological information; thus the documentation indirectly admitted the fetus' humanity:

> Since Planned Parenthood is the foremost abortion provider in the U.S., they have a responsibility to tell women the truth about fetal development and subsequent risks involved in pursuing abortion as an option. I know for a fact they do not. The baby is dehumanized as much as possible by being termed a "blob," "product of conception," or "uterine contents."[37]

Another woman recounted a similar case in the same *Federal Register* account:

> If I had known the reality of what I chose, I would not have chosen abortion. I killed my baby! How would you feel/react if someday several years after abortion you saw pictures of a 12-week-old fetus and learned that this was the picture of a perfectly formed human being. . . . [they] told me it was a "blob!" I was devastated beyond all description.[38]

Title X is a unique example: one can argue that those who formulated Title X specifically recognized the fetus as human.

The descriptions of violations of Title X, as noted in a 1988 *Federal Register,* included women's statements that the fetus was human.

In addition to Title X, other federal programs, such as Medicaid, have not permitted abortion funding. As a result of a 1980 case, *Harris v. McRae,* Congress is not required to fund abortions with Medicaid dollars.

4.7 The Rule Against Perpetuities (an inheritance/estate law)

There are other areas of law that touch upon the unborn, treating the fetus as, for all intents and purposes, a legal entity. The Rule Against Perpetuities, governing the "vesting" or the passing of estates, is one such area. The usual statement of this rule is: "An interest is void if there is *any possibility,* however remote, that the interest *may vest more than* 21 years after the death of persons alive at the creation of the interest."[39] Although the passing of an estate is contingent upon live birth, the Rule Against Perpetuities allows that "Any actual periods of gestation are included within the permissible perpetuities period. For purposes of the Rule a person is treated as in being from the time of conception."[40] In other words, someone can will inheritance to a fetus within the womb. In the case of Friday's Estate, the court stated that "The rule does not consider the persons in whom the interest shall vest, so long as vesting is within the period specified by law. . .They may be persons unborn when the trust is created."[41]

As demonstrated by the evidence above, legal evidence identifying the fetus as human has always existed within the legislation and courts of various nations. Accordingly, many justices, including some members of the current U.S. Supreme Court, affirm that the state has a compelling or necessary interest to protect the fetus' life.

Additionally, medical science has enabled man physically to observe the fetus as an identifiable human, even within the first trimester.

This evidence of the fetus' humanity leads to the question of the U.S. Supreme Court's current makeup: 1) Those who concur with modern scientific evidence that the fetus is human and, consequently, recognize a legitimate or compelling interest to prohibit the so-called right of abortion in all instances; 2) those who concur with modern scientific evidence that the fetus is human but provide the fetus protection only in certain instances; and 3) those who know modern scientific evidence but somehow conclude that the fetus' life is not a legitimate or compelling interest to prohibit abortion in any instance.

Some legal scholars contend that abortion on demand was established as a liberty based on a supposed "right to privacy" drawn from the Fourteenth Amendment. But can a liberty exist when another compelling interest, the fetus' life, is at stake?

5

Cultural Evidence

The fetus, though enclosed in the womb of its mother, is already a human being and it is a most monstrous crime to rob it of the life which it has not yet begun to enjoy. If it seems [more] horrible to kill a man in his own house than in a field, because a man's house is his place of most secure refuge, it ought surely to be deemed more atrocious to destroy a fetus in the womb before it has come to light.

—John Calvin[1]

5.1 Biblical Evidence Identifying Human Life Within the Womb

The writers of the Old and New Testaments recognized the humanity of the fetus. The Scriptures reveal plentiful evidence of the existence of human life within the womb, the growth of that life and the uniqueness of that life. The excerpts below verify the long-standing biblical belief that each fetus is a distinct human being.

5.1A The Existence of Human Life Within the Womb

Scripture identifies the fetus as a human being, referring to its bones, and treating the fetus as a child.

Bones in the Womb: *Ecclesiastes* 11:5

> As thou knowest not what is the way of the spirit, nor how
> the bones are joined together in the womb of her that is
> with child: so thou knowest not the works of God, who
> is the maker of all.

Notice the words "bones" mentioned by Solomon, to whom
Ecclesiastes is attributed. Solomon indicated that bones do grow
in the womb of her who is with child. A fetus' bones surely
do grow in the womb, as evidenced in medical studies and other
scientific data.

A Child Within the Womb: *Genesis* 25:22-25

Several Scripture passages refer to the fetus as a child within
the womb. For example, in the first book of the Old Testament,
Genesis, there are references to the children (sons) within
Rebecca's womb.

> But the children struggled in her womb: and she said: If
> it were to be so with me, what need was there to conceive?
> And she went to consult the Lord. And he answering said:
> Two nations are in thy womb, and two peoples shall be
> divided out of thy womb, and one people shall overcome
> the other, and the elder shall serve the younger. And when
> her time was come to be delivered, behold twins were
> found in her womb. He that came forth first was red, and
> hairy like a skin: and his name was called Esau. Immedi-
> ately the other coming forth, held his brother's foot in his
> hand, and therefore, he was called Jacob.

5.1B The Growth of Human Life Within the Womb: Isaias, Job

Several Old Testament passages refer to the growth of life
within the womb. Just as a child grows into adulthood, the boy
or girl within the womb grows into childhood. Some Old Testament references follow:

Isaias 44:2

> Thus saith the Lord that made and formed thee, thy helper
> from the womb: Fear not, O my servant Jacob, and thou
> most righteous whom I have chosen.

Job 31:15

> Did not he that made me in the womb make him also:
> and did not one and the same form me in the womb?

Isaias 49:1, 5

> . . .The Lord hath called me from the womb, from the
> bowels of my mother he hath been mindful of my
> name. . .And now saith the Lord, that formed me from the
> womb to be his servant. . .

5.1C The Unique Creation of Each Human Life:
Jeremias, Psalms

In the Bible, the womb is considered a sanctuary to protect
human life. Each human life represents a unique creation that
is violently stopped and unnaturally ended when abortion
occurs. The following Old Testament passages confirm the
unique creation of each human life conceived in the womb:

Jeremias 1:5

> Before I formed thee in the bowels of thy mother, I knew
> thee: and before thou camest forth out of the womb, I sanc-
> tified thee, and made thee a prophet unto the nations.

Psalm 138(139):13, 15-16

> . . .thou hast protected me from my mother's womb. . .My
> bone is not hidden from thee, which thou hast made in
> secret: and my substance in the lower parts of the earth.
> Thy eyes did see my imperfect being. . .

5.1D *New Testament Evidence of the Fetus' Humanity:* Galatians, Luke

The New Testament also refers to the unique human characteristics of each fetus created within the womb. The following New Testament Scripture passages reveal the humanity of each life within the womb:

Galatians 1:15,16

> But when it pleased him, who separated me from my mother's womb, and called me by his grace, to reveal his Son in me, that I might preach him among the Gentiles, immediately I condescended not to flesh and blood.

Luke 1:41

> And it came to pass, that when Elizabeth heard the salutation of Mary, the infant leaped in her womb. And Elizabeth was filled with the Holy Ghost.

5.2 An Overview of Traditional Judeo-Christian Beliefs

Historically, the fetus has always received protection within the Judeo-Christian tradition. Jewish and Christian beliefs focus on the fetus as a person. For instance, original Jewish and Christian documents view the fetus as a separate human being at conception. (Modern medical knowledge confirms that each human life begins at conception; the actual unique life begins when a sperm from a male unites with the egg of a female.) In order to describe the Judeo-Christian belief that the fetus is human, this section is divided into the following segments:

> Judaic Belief in the Humanity of the Fetus
> The Early Church's Recognition of the Humanity of the Fetus
> Life in the Womb Upheld by the Reformation
> The Belief of Religious Groups in the Humanity of the Unborn.

5.2A *Judaic Belief in the Humanity of the Fetus*

Both the Old Testament and Judaic law verify the belief in the humanity of the fetus. Old Testament Scripture passages, such as *Isaias* 44:2 and *Psalm* 138(139):13, 15-16, refer to the humanity of the fetus.

The following statement from author John T. Noonan confirms the historical Jewish belief in the humanity of the fetus:

> In classic Jewish law, abortion was permitted only to save the life of the mother. Life in this case was sacrificed for life. In the same way, in rabbinical responsa, it was permitted to break the Sabbath only to save a human life, and this exception was understood to include the life of an unborn child. The Chief Rabbi of Israel, following the tradition, described abortion in 1963 as "an appurtenance of murder."[2]

Most interesting is the fact that the Jewish Torah (the first five books of the Old Testament) says, in *Genesis* 9:6, "Whosoever shall shed man's blood, his blood shall be shed: for man was made to the image of God." Many orthodox rabbis have interpreted this passage to mean that "abortion is murder" since human blood is shed. (Indeed, every abortion sheds blood, and certainly it is not animal blood.) The table in Section 5.2D below includes Jewish beliefs on abortion. Note that Orthodox Jewish beliefs are the most long-standing beliefs in regard to the sanctity of life in the womb.

5.2B *The Early Church's Recognition of the Humanity of the Fetus*

Evidence shows that the early Christians fimly upheld the humanity of the fetus. John T. Noonan summarizes the early Christian Church's position:

> From the time the Christian Church had emerged in the Mediterranean world in the first century A.D., opposition to abortion had been one of its moral tenets and one of its most distinctive behavioral injunctions. The use and the

user of abortifacients were denounced in the New Testament itself. A first-century catechism, *The Teaching of the Twelve Apostles* [*The Didache*], placed those who are "killers of the child, who abort the mold of God," between murderers and adulterers, all embarked on "the Way of Darkness." The early Christian *Epistle of Barnabas* declared, "You shall not slay the child by abortions." The Greek Church and the Latin Church in the course of time developed specific sanctions against the sin.[3]

A 1986 letter to the *New York Times* further testified to the early Christian Church's belief in the humanity of the fetus. The letter states that the Christian sense, as echoed by St. Augustine, has always been that "the one about to be born must always be considered as one already born."[4]

The Catholic Catechism cites the *Epistle of Barnabas* (2:19): "Do not murder a child by abortion, or commit infanticide."[5] The same passage contains "two operative words in the prohibition," explicitly "murder" and "child."[6]

According to Tertullian, a writer in the early Church, an "induced abortion at any stage was a homicide."[7]

St. Basil confirmed the humanity of the fetus by stating: "A woman who deliberately destroys a fetus is answerable for murder. And any fine distinction as to its being formed or unformed is not admissible among us."[8]

Clement of Alexandria declared that abortion destroyed what God had created and violated the command to love one's neighbor.[9] As another example of the recognition of the humanity of the fetus, consider the following statement within a letter from the apologist Athenagoras to the Emperor Marcus Aurelius in A.D. 177: "All who use abortifacients are homicides and will account to God for their abortions as for the killing of men."[10] The Fathers of the Church unanimously maintained that children in the womb may not be murdered, and "no distinction is made between the earlier and later stages of gestation."[11]

5.2C Life in the Womb Upheld by the Reformation

Contrary to what much of the modern media may lead one

to believe, the Reformation, as represented by many of its major figures, continued the clear historical moral teaching that the fetus is human. Even on American soil, a Puritan named Benjamin Wadsworth, later a president of Harvard College, declared in his sermons, entitled *The Well-Ordered Family,* that those who would "destroy the Fruit of their Womb" are "guilty of Murder in God's account."[12]

Protestant denominations and leaders denouncing abortion have included the popular Anglican writer Dean W. R. Inge, who rejected abortion "as invoking the destruction of a life which had already begun."[13]Among others, the Church of England has historically been opposed to abortion. Other Protestant voices defending the fetus have included that of Helmut Thielicke, a Lutheran theologian who "pronounced abortion permissible only where a life had to be sacrificed to save the mother's life." The fetus, or life within the womb, was not to be eliminated for any pragmatic reasons. Thielicke wrote that, except for the rare case when a mother's life is endangered, the "genesis of human life is a sacrosanct domain which dare not to be invaded by human hands or 'rationalized,' that is, subjected to utilitarian considerations."[14]

To summarize the Reformation thinking throughout the past several hundred years: Protestant leaders have defended the fetus as a human life and viewed abortion as the destruction of that life.

5.2D *Belief of Religious Groups in the Humanity of the Unborn*

The list below summarizes the positions of many religious organizations today on abortion and consequently verifies the fact that some Protestant denominations shifted from a liberal, pro-abortion view to a moderate or conservative position during the 1980's. Jewish beliefs are also summarized. Orthodox Jewish believers, although perhaps not as strict as Catholicism and the Eastern Orthodox churches, have kept a long-held belief that the fetus must not be aborted on demand. The fact that some denominations withdrew their liberal support of abortion is additional evidence for the humanity of the fetus.

Major Religious Organizations' Abortion Positions: 1979,[15] 1989

Conservative: Ranges from prohibition of all abortions to the tolerance of abortion for incest, rape, or to save the mother's life. Against abortion on demand.

Moderate: Allows abortion—generally first trimester only—for economic, physical, emotional, and social considerations in addition to rape, incest, and to save the mother's life.

Moderate to liberal: Supports abortion on demand. Few limitations, although some groups oppose late-term abortions.

African Methodist Church:
   1979—conservative; 1989—conservative.
American Baptist Assn.: 1979—conservative;
   1989—conservative.
American Baptist Church in U.S.A.:
   1979—moderate; 1989—moderate. Denounced "irresponsible sexual behaviour" adding annually to large number of abortions.[16]
American Lutheran Church (merged into the Evangelical Lutheran Church of America):
   1979—moderate; 1989—moderate. Toughened its stand in 1980, declaring that abortion "ends a unique human life."[17]
Assemblies of God: 1979—conservative; 1989—conservative.
Baptist Bible Fellowship:
   1979—conservative; 1989—conservative.
Christian Churches: 1979—conservative; 1989—conservative.
Churches of Christ: 1979—conservative; 1989—conservative.
Disciples of Christ:
   1979—moderate to liberal; 1989—moderate to liberal.
Eastern Orthodox Churches:
   1979—conservative; 1989—conservative.
Episcopal Church: 1979—moderate to liberal; 1989—moderate. Now opposes abortion as a means of birth control, family planning, sex selection and convenience.[18]
Judaism (Conservative): 1979—moderate; 1989—moderate.
Judaism (Orthodox): 1979—conservative; 1989—conservative.

Judaism (Reform):
  1979—moderate to liberal: 1989—moderate to liberal.
Lutheran Church, Missouri Synod:
  1979—conservative; 1989—conservative.
Lutheran Church in America:
  1979—moderate: 1989—moderate.
National Baptist Convention, U.S.A.:
  1979—conservative; 1989—conservative.
National Association of Evangelicals:
  1979—conservative; 1989—conservative.
Presbyterian Church in U.S.:
  1979—moderate; 1989—moderate. Stated that abortion "should not be used for convenience or...birth control."[19]
Roman Catholic Church:
  1979—conservative; 1989—conservative.
Southern Baptist Convention: 1979—conservative; 1989—conservative. Opposes abortion except to save mother's life.
United Church of Christ:
  1979—moderate to liberal; 1989—moderate to liberal.
United Methodist Church:
  1979—moderate to liberal; 1989—moderate. Opposes abortion as means of birth control or gender selection.
United Presbyterian Church:
  1979—moderate to liberal; 1989—moderate to liberal.

Mainline Protestant Opposition to Abortion

Despite attempts to label the Pro-Life Movement as solely a Catholic issue, much evidence indicates that mainline Protestant churches in the twentieth century have also affirmed that the fetus is a unique human that consequently must be protected. According to John T. Noonan, "In the twentieth century the Protestant opposition to abortion was equally manifest."[20]

At the time of *Roe v. Wade,* many Protestant churches, such as the Churches of Christ, considered abortion what its previous legal definition was in many states, that is, murder. The press seldom reported on the Protestant churches that opposed abortion, and the majority of the media attempted to galvanize the issue or desensitize the American people by characterizing the Pro-Life Movement as a purely Catholic force, thus playing on an historic anti-Catholic sentiment in America. However, life in the womb, with all of the medical and scientific verifications, cannot logically be a purely Catholic issue. The following Protestant churches were among many that at the time of *Roe v. Wade* considered the fetus a human being and, consequently, protected its life:

Churches of Christ: Abortion is "murder," except possibly to preserve the life of the mother.[21]

American Baptist Association: Abortion breaks divine law and is "an act of sin and wickedness."[22]

Baptist Bible Fellowship: Abortion is "a slaughter of the innocents." Government is "ignoring God's laws and will be judged."[23]

Since *Roe v. Wade,* many liberal Protestant denominations or groups have shifted to the right, recognizing the humanity of the fetus. Many recent newspaper articles have appeared on the moderation of previous liberal abortion attitudes among the "mainline" denominations. For example, an article entitled "Protestants Modify Stance on Abortion" noted several instances where major Protestant denominations had modified their "pro-choice" or pro-abortion position or, in some cases, reversed it. George W. Cornell stated: "Most major Protestant denominations which once widely condoned abortion now either oppose it or specify limitations to it."[24] As a whole, liberal Protestant churches, while struggling to maintain the "right" to abortion, also recognize that abortion denies the right to life of another individual.

Eastern Orthodox Opposition to Abortion

The Eastern Orthodox Church, which separated from the Roman Catholic Church around A.D. 1000, also maintains that abortion is murder.

Catholic Opposition to Abortion

The Catholic Church's perennial opposition to abortion also adds to the tremendous religious evidence that shows the fetus to be human. Throughout the twentieth century, as throughout her entire history, the Catholic Church has condemned abortion. For example, current laws within the Catholic Church state that abortion is not only the "expulsion of the immature fetus," but is "the killing of the same fetus in any way and at any time from the moment of conception."[25] The Catholic Church clearly indicates that abortion is "killing," thus indicating the taking of a human life.

The Catholic Church today, although frustrated by the many liberal "Catholics" who condone abortion, remains absolutely opposed to abortion. Hundreds of Catholic documents dating from the first century through the present testify to the same moral doctrine.[26] Perhaps Mother Teresa of Calcutta best expresses the existence of life in the womb and the need for the accompanying defense of that life by the Catholic Church and others:

> The greatest destroyer of peace today is the cry of the innocent, unborn child. For if a mother can murder her own child in her own womb, what is left but for you and me to kill each other?[27]

Pope John Paul II, while visiting America in the 1980's, gave the following succinct summary of the humanity of the fetus:

> Every human person, no matter how vulnerable or helpless, no matter how young or how old, no matter how healthy, handicapped or sick, no matter how useful or productive for society, is a being of inestimable worth, created in the image and likeness of God. This is the dignity of America, the reason she exists, the condition for her survival, yes, the ultimate test of her greatness: to respect every human person, especially the weakest and most defenseless ones, those as yet unborn.[28]

6

Social Evidence

Social concern for the fetus is increasing. This concern is more evidence that the fetus is human. Why else would so many diverse groups—Catholic, Protestant, Jewish, even atheist—join together to protest abortion?

Outrage about abortion is gaining steam in ever-increasing proportions. The year 1988 can be considered the beginning of another civil war, a war in which Evangelicals and Catholics, among others, joined forces in non-violent blockades outside abortion facilities. Perhaps the best explanation of this outrage is as follows: "Abortion is barbaric; it's tyranny," said Randall Terry, founder of Operation Rescue.[1] Operation Rescue is a national coalition formed to stage protests and blockades at locations where abortions are performed.

Social upheaval over abortion began escalating tremendously as of 1988. The humanity of the fetus, often ignored by the media, received greater attention beginning that year. Operation Rescue grabbed national headlines while staging massive sit-ins (blockades) at abortion facilities nationwide. A year later, news coverage included the U.S. Supreme Court's 1989 *Webster v. Reproductive Health Services* case, which upheld the legality of some abortion restrictions. In this landmark case, the Supreme Court ruled that states may impose restrictions on abortion, including the denial of public money, public medical personnel, or public facilities for abortion.

Social unrest about abortion stems, in part, from the tremendous biological evidence that the fetus is human.

The following social evidence is discussed below:

> The Increase in Media Coverage
> The Rise in Demonstrations
> Civil Disobedience in Support of the Unborn
> Statistical Evidence
> Presidential Opposition to Abortion on Demand
> Public Belief in the Humanity of the Fetus
> Beliefs Reflected in Language

6.1 The Increase in Media Coverage

Many recent abortion headlines grew out of increasing tension surrounding the belief that the fetus is human. Sit-ins, protests, and pro-life court decisions began escalating in the 1980's. For example, the U.S. Supreme Court allowed states to restrict abortion as of 1989.

The abortion issue appeared on the front and inside pages of major newspapers and magazines in greater frequency beginning in the late 1980's, indicating that the question of the humanity of the fetus is now a large concern in society.

The following are sample titles of news stories that appeared in 1988 and 1989:

"Pro-Life Forces on the Offensive," *Washington Times,* August 29, 1988.

"Abortion: America's New Civil War," *U.S. News & World Report,* October 3, 1988.

"Atlanta Police Use Tougher Tactics as Abortion Foes Return to Streets," *Washington Post,* October 4, 1988.

"Prison Term Fails to Crush Resolve of Pro-Life Activist," *Washington Times,* December 13, 1988.

"Bush Wants Abortion Laws 'Overturned,' " *USA Today,* January 24, 1989.

"March for Life Attracts 65,000," *Washington Times,* January 24, 1989.

"Reluctant Couple Converts to Activism," *Washington Post,* February 2, 1989.

"Save the Babies," *Time,* May 1, 1989.

"Supreme Court Restricts Right to Abortion, Giving States Wide Latitude for Regulation," *Washington Post,* July 4, 1989.

6.2 The Rise in Demonstrations

Demonstrations against abortion increased dramatically as of 1988 with the emergence of massive national protests. Demonstrations against legal abortion have existed at least since the *Roe v. Wade* decision in 1973. However, media attention did not heavily focus on these protests until the recent massive sit-ins at abortion facilities. Operation Rescue, which includes conservative Catholics and Evangelicals, has grown tremendously since the initial mass arrests (outside of abortion facilities) in 1988. For example, Operation Rescue sit-in locations swelled from 30 cities in 1988 to 130 cities in October 1989.

Though largely ignored or misrepresented by the media, at least 350,000 people gathered in Washington, D.C., in April of 1990 for a rally supporting the protection of life in the womb. *Objective aerial views of the crowd, yet to be shown by many news organizations, indicate that this rally was perhaps the largest protest ever in Washington, D.C.!* One of the most consistent indicators of the numbers participating in demonstrations to protect the fetus is the March for Life in Washington, D.C., each January. In 1993, the press estimated at least 75,000 participants in the march. (Police and other eyewitnesses reported 225,000-300,000.) In addition, thousands of protests outside hospitals and abortion facilities have occurred since abortion was legalized in 1973. These protests have occurred in all 50 states. An example is the Fairfax Hospital protests.

This Virginia hospital was still performing abortions in 1989, and has been the location of a number of protests against abortion. At the February 25, 1989, protest, according to a news report, "more than 1000 demonstrators—including Redskins Coach Joe Gibbs and players Darrell Green, Keith Griffin and Charles Mann—converged Saturday at Fairfax County Hospital to protest its policy on abortions."[2] One football player said, concerning a film of an abortion: "I looked at the violence of it; it was so ugly and so gruesome."[3] The "pro-choice" movement was present, too, though represented by only a handful of protestors for their cause. There were a very few pro-abortion advocates with signs (for example, a sign in bold letters read, "Keep Abortion Legal"). But many banners in the crowd had pictures of aborted fetuses—*pictorial, factual arguments.* Some others read, "Thou Shalt Not Kill," "The Gift of Life, God's Special Gift," and "Rescue Those Who Are Unjustly Sentenced to Death." Many protestors sang hymns, pleading for an end to abortion. At the same demonstration, one lady held the aborted bodies of Esther and Grace, whose photographs appear in Chapter 2. Open to the public eye were the bodies of these two dead, aborted baby girls, one a victim of a salt-poisoning abortion in the 19th week of pregnancy, the other a victim of a prostaglandin abortion in the 24th week of pregnancy. Each had a definite head, ears, nose, mouth, eyes, rib cage, feet, hands, etc. This local protest, similar to demonstrations in other communities, provided physical evidence as to the humanity of the fetus.

6.3 Civil Disobedience in Support of the Unborn

The increase of civil disobedience—that is, sit-ins or "Rescues" and ensuing arrests at abortion facilities—further verifies the widespread social belief that the fetus is human.

Perhaps the best example of this growing civil disobedience is seen in Joan Andrews (Joan Andrews Bell, since her marriage in 1991), considered by some to be a modern-day Joan of Arc. She was responsible for the first "Rescue" operation in Florida.

She believes that it is her call to express what she says is an obligation to obey a higher law, much in the same way that the German people had a commitment to disobey laws that allowed Jews to be killed.[4] She told Richard Dujardin of the *Washington Times*:

> I'm...at the point in my life where I know that God's will is all that matters. And if that means going to jail again for trying to stop the killing of babies—if it means laying down my life—that's how it will have to be. Believe me, I dread going back to prison. But we have to remain faithful to God.[5]

Joan Andrews' participation in blockades of abortion clinics, involving a large number of arrests due to her committed love for the unborn, has inspired others to do the same—thousands of men and women have followed suit. There is no doubt that part of society is crying out against what they believe to be the taking of human life.

An October 4, 1988 *Washington Post* report on sit-ins at abortion facilities in Atlanta included the following:

> Police made more than 360 arrests today in the second round of efforts by abortion foes to focus national attention on their protests here as they blocked entrances to three abortion clinics.[6]

In the same article, Michael McGonagle, a leader from Operation Rescue, stated:

> Atlanta is trying to send a message to pro-life rescuers that they'll get tough, and we'll go away...What we're trying to say is, "Get tough with us, and we'll stay."[7]

Atlanta became a focal point for sit-ins against abortion. By October 5, 1988, Atlanta police had arrested 754 people during protests; most protestors remained imprisoned only a few days, but 48 remained in jail from July 19 until August 27, and nine protestors remained in jail through at least October 5, 1988.[8]

Another story, entitled "153 Arrested in Abortion Protest at D.C. Clinic," reported that "close to 300 protestors ringed the Hillcrest Women's Surgi-Center at 7603 Georgia Avenue, NW"[9] at a Rescue there in 1989. According to the report, "about half of the demonstrators sat down in front of the doors to the building, preventing patients and staff from going in and out. Despite police orders, the protestors refused to leave."[10]

Several blockades of abortion facilities occurred in the Washington, D.C. area on the same day. The intensity, frequency and conviction of ordinary citizens' participation in Rescues and blockades indicates a strong belief that the fetus is human. One woman who participated in the Hillcrest Rescue said, "We are attempting to close down the abortion clinic to save the lives of unborn children." Her conviction seemed intense as she added: "We are determined that no abortion will take place today."[11] She said that some crimes (meaning abortion) are "so heinous that you have to take action."[12]

In 1988, syndicated columnist Cal Thomas effectively summarized this new wave of civil disobedience:

> Pro-Life forces, frustrated by 15 years of abortion on demand and their inability to halt the practice, are increasingly borrowing an effective tactic of the 1960's left—civil disobedience.[13]

Thomas cited several key points that illustrate the strength of non-violent sit-ins on behalf of the lives of the unborn, noting that nearly 5,000 citizens had been arrested between May and August, 1988 for trespassing on the grounds of abortion facilities in several U.S. cities. In August, 1988, just as the civil disobedience movement was about to mushroom, Thomas stated:

> If Operation Rescue catches fire and goes national, politicians will have to take note. The key is those conservative ministers. If they take up the cause of civil disobedience and encourage those who have been comfortable in their church pews too long to empty into the streets, profound change on abortion will come. Surely the jails could not

hold them all. And our society could no longer ignore their
message that what is taking place behind "clinic" doors
is the slaughter of innocent human beings.[14]

In the ensuing year there was a dramatic increase in the number of blockades of abortion facilities.[15] In May, 1988, fewer
than 100 sit-ins occurred at abortion facilities in 30 cities. In
October of 1989, 502 took place in 130 cities. There were
approximately 2,000 arrests at the blockades in May, 1988; in
October, 1989 the number was 34,429. (At least 15,000 more
participated in blockades, but were not arrested.) These figures
represent a staggering increase in activity for Operation Rescue
and similar organizations.

6.4 Statistical Evidence

Statistics alone cannot prove or disprove the humanity of the
fetus. However, statistics can, when coupled with tremendous
social, medical, or other evidence, serve as a barometer to indicate the seriousness of abortion. The lives of a tremendous number of unique beings, with human genetic makeup complete at
conception, are being ended by abortion.

From 1.5 to 1.6 million fetuses are legally aborted each year
in the United States alone, and 55 million worldwide. One-third
of all pregnancies end in abortion in the United States. The rate
of abortion has quadrupled in America since 1973. More abortions than live births occur in Washington, D.C.

The 25 million legal abortions performed in the United States
between 1973 and 1990 equaled the population of Canada as
of 1990, as illustrated on page 73. The overwhelming majority
of these abortions were done for the sake of convenience.

CANADA

U.S.

Population of Canada
as of January, 1990

equal to

Total Number of Legal
Abortions Performed
in the United States
Between 1973 and 1990

6.5 Presidential Opposition to Abortion on Demand

For at least a decade, America's presidents supported the repeal of legalized abortion on demand and, consequently, strengthened the belief in the humanity of the fetus. Former President Ronald Reagan defended the fetus and its humanity in a book entitled *Abortion and the Conscience of the Nation.* While in office, he petitioned the Supreme Court to reverse *Roe v. Wade.*

President George Bush, following in the path of Ronald Reagan, also opposed abortion. As Vice President, while running for President, he stated, "I oppose abortion, I oppose Federal funding for abortion. I want to see the *Roe v. Wade* decision changed so that it won't legalize abortion...."[16] During the 1988 presidential election campaign, candidates debated the abortion issue, reflecting the increasing public concern over abortion on demand. The 1992 campaigns also focused on the question of abortion, with the right to life of the unborn being a prominent issue in many races.

6.6 Public Belief in the Humanity of the Fetus

Public recognition of the humanity of the fetus is evident in recent social commentary. The following statements appeared in *USA Today* after that paper asked its readers if state abortion laws should be changed:

> I challenge USA TODAY to print a picture of a baby 15 to 20 weeks old. I also challenge the paper to print a picture of that same baby once it has been aborted. And then I challenge someone to tell me that it isn't murder.[17]

Another individual wrote:

> The sound of all those voices clamoring for and against abortion is drowned out in my mind by the silent screams of millions of innocent children murdered for the convenience of their mothers.[18]

6.7 Beliefs Reflected in Language

Evidence of popular belief of the human life of the fetus appears in the idioms of the English language:

"Eating for two" is an expression often used to refer to the eating habits of a pregnant woman.

A woman who has had a miscarriage is said to have "lost her baby."

An ultrasound reveals whether the fetus is male or female. The results are described: "It's a boy," or "It's a girl." The picture shows the baby's nose, ears, head, body, etc.

Media and society warn expectant mothers not to take alcohol or smoke while pregnant or the baby might be harmed; however, the same media and society often condone the destruction of the fetus if the woman does not want it.

A recent newspaper article highlights the entrenched social belief, despite the present abortion-on-demand policies, that a baby exists within the womb of a pregnant woman:

> Starting with the moment you learn you're pregnant, your baby will change your life. . . . Many doctors believe that a glass of wine on a special occasion would not damage the baby. But the medical facts are that when you drink, the alcohol passes through your system and into your baby's. And no one knows at what level, if any, alcohol is safe for the baby.[19]

The article excerpted above was written by a physician, using the word "baby" in reference to the fetus in the womb. The article continued: "This doesn't mean that a woman who had a drink or two in the weeks before she knew she was pregnant has harmed her baby."[20]

The decision whether to use the term "fetus" or "baby" seems simply to indicate whether the speaker esteems the new life or condones abortion. It seems to reflect attitudes and value judgments rather than scientific fact.

John O. Anderson wrote, "America has. . . become mired in a war of words, lost in a semantic smokescreen that clouds the real issues."[21] He concluded that pro-choice, rights, viability, wantedness—are not real issues. "They are modern diversions—and even anti-abortionists have been caught up in them, trying to argue their own side and win."[22]

Is the fetus human? The answer to this question is not difficult. Both the hard scientific data and the evidence from many other aspects of human life give a clear reply.

The real question is: Does every human being have the right to life?

Notes by Chapters

Chapter 1: Biological Evidence

1. Bernard Nathanson, M.D., *Aborting America* (Garden City, NY: Doubleday, 1979), pp. 174-175.
2. *Akron v. Akron Center for Reproductive Health,* 462 U.S. 416 at 458.
3. Melody Green, "Children...Things We Throw Away?" (Lyndale, TX: Pretty Good Printing, 1986), p. 2.
4. Ibid.
5. Bob Larson, *Larson's Book of Family Issues* (Wheaton, IL: Tyndale House, 1986), p. 297.
6. Ibid.
7. Landrum B. Shettles, M.D., and David Rorvik, "Human Life Begins at Conception," in *Rites of Life* (Grand Rapids, MI: Zondervan, 1983), cited in *Abortion: Opposing Viewpoints* (St. Paul, MN: Greenhaven Press, 1986), p. 16.
8. Ibid.
9. Ibid., p. 17.
10. Ibid.
11. Ibid.
12. Ibid.
13. Ibid., pp. 17-18.
14. Larson, p. 297.
15. Sally B. Olds, et al., *Obstetric Nursing* (Menlo Park, CA: Addison-Wesley Publishing, 1980), p. 136.
16. Shettles, p. 19.
17. Ibid.
18. Bernard Nathanson, cited in the film *Massacre of Innocence* (Gainesville, FL: Reel to Real Ministries).
19. Bernard Nathanson, cited in *Abortion: A Reflection on Life* (Ft. Lauderdale, FL: Coral Ridge Ministries, 1989), p. 5.
20. Nathanson, *Aborting America,* p. 164.

Is the Fetus Human?

21. Hymie Gordon, cited in the film *Massacre of Innocence.*
22. *California Medicine,* cited in the film *Massacre of Innocence.*
23. Alan Guttmacher, et al., *Planning Your Family* (New York: Macmillan, 1964), p. 28.
24. Paul Rockwell, M.D., "Consider This Observation by a New York Doctor," Pregnancy Center brochure, 1988.
25. D. James Kennedy, *Abortion, a Reflection on Life* (Ft. Lauderdale, FL: Coral Ridge Ministries, 1989), p. 4.
26. Suzanne M. Rini, *Beyond Abortion: A Chronicle of Fetal Experimentation* (Avon, NJ: Magnificat Press, 1988; TAN, 1993), p. 162.
27. A. W. Liley, "The Foetus as a Personality," in *Australian and New Zealand Journal of Psychiatry,* Vol. 6, No. 2 (June, 1972), pp. 99-100.
28. Ibid., p. 100.
29. Ibid., pp. 100-101.
30. Ibid.
31. Ibid., p. 103.
32. Ibid.
33. Ibid., pp. 103-104.
34. H. B. Valman and J. F. Pearson, "What the Fetus Feels," *British Medical Journal,* Jan. 26, 1980, p. 233.
35. Ibid.
36. Ibid.
37. Ibid., p. 234.
38. Ibid.
39. Ibid., p. 233.
40. Ibid.
41. Ibid.
42. Ibid.
43. Ibid., p. 234.
44. Mary Meehan, "The Ex-Abortionists: They Have Confronted the Reality," *Washington Post,* April 1, 1988, p. A21.
45. Ibid.
46. Ibid.
47. Ibid.
48. Olga Fairfax, "101 Uses for a Dead (or Alive) Baby," *ALL About Issues,* Jan. 1984, pp. 6-7.
49. Ibid., p. 7.
50. Ibid.
51. Ibid., p. 9.
52. Rini, p. 27.
53. Ibid., p. 28.
54. Ibid., p. 33.
55. Ibid., p. 34.
56. Ibid., p. 36.
57. Ibid., p. 39.

58. Ibid.
59. Fairfax, p. 8.
60. Ibid.
61. Rini, p. 33.
62. Fairfax, pp. 8-9.
63. Ibid., p. 9.
64. Rini, pp. 119-160.
65. Ibid., p. 42.
66. Ibid., p. 44.
67. Ibid.
68. Ibid., p. 42.
69. Ibid., p. 43.
70. Ibid.
71. Ibid., p. 74.
72. Ibid., p. 76.
73. Ibid., p. 76-78.
74. Ibid., p. 81.
75. Ibid.

Chapter 3: Emotional Evidence

1. Dr. and Mrs. J. C. Willke, *Abortion...Questions and Answers* (Cincinnati: Hayes Publishing, 1985), p. 124.
2. Willke citing I. Kent ("Abortion Has a Profound Impact," *Family Practice News,* June 1980, p. 80), p. 124.
3. Ibid.
4. D. James Kennedy, *Abortion: Reflection on Life* (Ft. Lauderdale, FL: Coral Ridge Ministries, 1989), p. 13.
5. Ibid.
6. Ibid., p. 12.
7. Willke citing C. Tishler ("Adolescent Suicide Attempt: Anniversary Reaction," *Pediatrics,* Vol. 68, 1981, pp. 670-671), p. 126.
8. Randall Terry, *Operation Rescue* (Springdale, PA: Whitaker House, 1989), p. 276.
9. Willke citing R. Kumar & K. Robson (*Psychol. Med.,* Vol. 8, 1978, pp. 711-715), p. 131.
10. Kennedy, p. 13.
11. Terry, pp. 273-274.
12. Kennedy, p. 12.
13. Willke citing J. Spaulding and J. Cavernar ("Psychosis Following Therapeutic Abortion," *Amer. Jour. Psychiatry,* Vol. 135, No. 3, March 1978, p. 364), p. 131.
14. Judie Brown, *Choices in Matters of Life and Death* (Avon, NJ: Magnificat Press, 1987), p. 33.

15. "A Man's Viewpoint on Abortion," *Great Expectations,* Fall 1988, Newsletter of the Rockville (MD) Pregnancy Center, pp. 1, 4.
16. Ibid., p. 1.
17. Ibid.
18. Ibid.
19. Ibid.
20. Ibid.
21. Ibid., p. 4.
22. Ibid.
23. Sallie Tisdale, "We Do Abortions Here," *Harper's Magazine,* Oct. 1987, p. 66.
24. Ibid.
25. Ibid., p. 67.
26. Dudley Clendinen, "The Abortion Conflict: What It Does to One Doctor," *New York Times Magazine,* Aug. 11, 1985, p. 26.
27. Ibid., pp. 26-28.
28. Magda Denes, *In Necessity and Sorrow: Life and Death at an Abortion Hospital* (New York: Basic Books, 1976).
29. Jim Edwards, "Ultrasound Videotape Shows Unborn in Death Throes," *Union Leader,* Nov. 20, 1984.
30. Willke citing N. Kaltreider et al. ("The Impact of Midtrimester Abortion Techniques on Patients and Staff," *Amer. Jour. Ob/Gyn,* Vol. 135, 1979, p. 235), p. 195.
31. Willke citing J. Roaks and W. Cates ("Emotional Impact of D&E vs. Instillation," *Family Planning Perspective,* Dec. 1977, pp. 276-277), p. 195.
32. Willke citing W. Hern ("Meeting of Amer. Assoc. Planned Parenthood Physicians," *Ob/Gyn News,* 1978), p. 196.

Chapter 4: Legal Evidence

1. Augustus B. Granville, *Sudden Death* (London: John Churchill, 1854).
2. *Roe v. Wade,* 410 U.S. 113 (1973) at 159.
3. Ibid., at 163.
4. 109 S. Ct. 3040 (1989).
5. Henry de Bracton, *On the Laws and Customs of England,* trans. by Samuel E. Thorne, Vol. 2 (Cambridge, MA: Harvard University Press, 1968), p. 341.
6. William Blackstone, *Commentaries on the Laws of England,* Book 1, Chap. 1 [London, 1803], (New York: Augustus Kelley Publishers, 1969), Facsimile Ed., p. 129.
7. Ibid., pp. 129-130.
8. Horatio Storer, *On Criminal Abortion in America* (Philadelphia: Lippincott, 1860), p. 12.
9. U.K. Statutes at Large, 43 Geo 3, c. 58 (758), p. 1804.

10. U.K. Statutes at Large, 9 and 10 Geo 4, c. 31 (374); c. 34 (770), p. 1829.
11. Storer, p. 77.
12. John T. Noonan, *A Private Choice* (New York: The Free Press, 1979), p. 5.
13. Ibid., p.6.
14. Mark A. Siegel, et al., eds., *Abortion: An Eternal Moral and Social Issue* (Wylie, TX: Information Plus, 1990), p. 4.
15. Compiled Statutes of Connecticut, 1854, pp. 307-308.
16. Code of Virginia, 1849, c. 191, p. 724.
17. Noonan, p. 52.
18. Storer, p. 12.
19. Ibid., pp. 86-87.
20. Dr. and Mrs. John Willke, *Abortion... Questions and Answers* (Cincinnati: Hayes Publishing, 1985), p. 15.
21. AMA Committee on Criminal Abortion, "22 Trans. of the Amer. Med. Assn. 258 (1871)," cited in *Roe v. Wade* at 142.
22. Noonan, pp. 33-34.
23. Ibid., p. 6.
24. Congressman Jacob Howard, 36th *Congressional Globe,* Vol. 36, Washington, D.C., May 23, 1866, p. 2766.
25. Robert A. Destro, "Abortion and the Constitution: The Need for a Life-Protective Amendment," *California Law Review* 63 (1975): 1250, 1286.
26. *Roe v. Wade,* 410 U.S. 113 (1973) at 163.
27. *Thornburgh v. Amer. Coll. of Obstetrics & Gynecology,* 476 U.S. 747 at 792.
28. *Akron v. Akron Center for Reproductive Health,* 462 U.S. 416 at 458.
29. "Geneticist Says Embryos Are 'Tiny Human Beings,' " *Washington Times,* Aug. 11, 1989, p. A2.
30. Cynthia Gorney, "Court Gives Woman Custody of 7 Embryo Children," *Washington Post,* Sept. 22, 1989, p. A13.
31. Noonan, p. 16.
32. *Byrn v. New York City Health and Hospitals Corp.,* 31 NY 2nd 207 at 398.
33. Ibid., 205 at 397.
34. Sect. 1008 of Title X, 42 USC 300a-6, in *Federal Register,* Vol. 53, No. 21, Feb. 2, 1988, p. 2922.
35. Ibid.
36. Ibid.
37. Ibid., p. 2924.
38. Ibid.
39. Jesse Dukeminier, *Future Interests,* 2nd ed. (New York: Gilbert Law Summaries, Harcourt Brace Jovanovich, 1979), p. 85.
40. Ibid., p. 87.
41. *Re Friday's Estate,* 313 PA 328 (1933), p. 333.

Chapter 5: Cultural Evidence

1. "So Says John Calvin," *Great Expectations,* Fall 1988 edition (Rockville, MD: Rockville Pregnancy Center), p. 1.
2. John T. Noonan, *A Private Choice* (New York: The Free Press, 1979), p. 62.
3. Ibid., p. 59.
4. Rev. Russell DeSimone, "St. Augustine, Too, Opposed Abortion," *New York Times,* March 29, 1986, p. 20.
5. John A. Hardon, *The Catholic Catechism* (Garden City, NY: Doubleday, 1975), p. 335.
6. Ibid.
7. Ibid.
8. Ibid., p. 338.
9. *Presbeia peri Christianon*, 35, quoted in Ibid., p. 339.
10. Ibid.
11. C. Coppens, "Abortion," *The Catholic Encyclopedia* (New York: Encyclopedia Press, 1913).
12. Noonan, p. 59.
13. Ibid., p. 60.
14. Ibid.
15. Bernard Nathanson, M.D., *Aborting America* (Garden City, NY: Doubleday, 1979), pp. 294-303.
16. George W. Cornell, "Protestants Modify Stance on Abortion," *Herald-Mail,* Aug. 5, 1989, p. A6.
17. Ibid.
18. Ibid.
19. Ibid.
20. Noonan, p. 60.
21. Nathanson, p. 295.
22. Ibid.
23. Ibid.
24. Cornell, p. A6.
25. Greg Erlandson, "Church Authorities Clarify Legal Definition of Abortion," *Arlington Catholic Herald,* Dec. 1, 1988, p. 1.
26. John A. Hardon, S.J., *Modern Catholic Dictionary* (Garden City: Doubleday, 1980), p. 5.
27. Cited in D. James Kennedy, *Abortion: A Reflection on Life* (Ft. Lauderdale, FL: Coral Ridge Ministries, 1989), p. 2.
28. "Stern Words by the Pope on Abortion," *New York Times,* Sept. 20, 1987, p. 31.

Chapter 6: Social Evidence

1. Randall Terry, interview with the author outside the U.S. Supreme Court, Jan. 23, 1989.

2. Matthew Scully, "Abortion Protest Attracts Thousand," *Washington Times,* Feb. 27, 1989, p. B3.

3. Ibid.

4. Richard Dujardin, "Prison Term Fails to Crush Resolve of Pro-Life Activist," *Washington Times,* Dec. 13, 1988, p. A10.

5. Ibid., p. A1.

6. Morris Thompson, "Atlanta Police Use Tougher Tactics as Abortion Foes Return to Streets," *Washington Post,* Oct. 5, 1988, p. A3.

7. Ibid.

8. Ibid.

9. Michael Abramowitz, "153 Arrested in Abortion Protest at D.C. Clinic," *Washington Post,* Jan. 24, 1989, p. B1.

10. Ibid.

11. Ibid.

12. Ibid., p. B3.

13. Cal Thomas, "Pro-Life Forces on the Offensive," syndicated columnist for the *Los Angeles Times,* printed in the Washington Times, Aug. 29, 1988, p. E3.

14. Ibid.

15. Tara Kritzer, SuAnne Carver, telephone interviews with Operation Rescue office, Binghamton, NY, Sept. 19, 1989, and Oct. 16, 1989.

16. Gerald Boyd, "Bush, in Iowa, Clarifies Stand on Legal Abortions," *New York Times,* Oct. 7, 1988.

17. "Change State Abortion Laws?" *USA Today,* July 7, 1989, p. 11A.

18. Ibid.

19. Robert Park, M.D., "Alcohol Can Cause Problems During Pregnancy," *Germantown* (MD) *Gazette,* April 12, 1989, p. B-19.

20. Ibid.

21. John O. Anderson, *Cry of the Innocents* (South Plainfield, NJ: Bridge, 1984), p. 56.

22. Ibid., p. 74.

Bibliography

Books

Anderson, John O. *Cry of the Innocents.* South Plainfield, NJ; Bridge, 1984.

Blackstone, William. *Commentaries on the Laws of England.* Facsimile edition. New York: Augustus Kelley Publishers, 1969.

de Bracton, Henry. *On the Laws and Customs of England.* Translated by Samuel E. Thorne. Vol. 2. Cambridge, MA: Harvard University Press, 1968.

Brown, Judie & Paul. *Choices in Matters of Life and Death.* Avon, NJ: Magnificat Press, 1987.

Christian, Rickly S. *The Woodland Hills Tragedy.* Westchester, IL: Crossway, 1985.

Coppens, C. "Abortion." *The Catholic Encyclopedia.* New York: Encyclopedia Press, 1913.

Denes, Magda. *In Necessity and Sorrow: Life and Death at an Abortion Hospital.* New York: Basic Books, 1976.

Dukeminier, Jesse. *Future Interests.* New York: Harcourt Brace Jovanovich, 1979.

Granville, Augustus B. *Sudden Death.* London: John Churchill, 1854.

Guttmacher, Alan F., Winfield Best, and Frederick S. Jaffe. *Planning Your Family.* New York: Macmillan, 1964.

Hardon, John A., S.J. *The Catholic Catechism.* Garden City, NY: Doubleday, 1975.

Hardon, John A., S.J. *Modern Catholic Dictionary.* Garden City, NY: Doubleday, 1980.

Kennedy, D. James. *Abortion: A Reflection On Life.* Ft. Lauderdale, FL: Coral Ridge Ministries, 1989.

Larson, Bob. *Larson's Book of Family Issues.* Wheaton, IL: Tyndale, 1986.

Nathanson, Bernard, M.D. *Aborting America.* Garden City, NY: Doubleday, 1979.

Noonan, John R. *A Private Choice.* New York: The Free Press, 1979.

Olds, Sally B., Marcia L. London, Patricia A. Ladewig, and Sharon V. Davidson. *Obstetric Nursing.* Menlo Park, CA: Addison-Wesley Publishing, 1980.

Reagan, Ronald. *Abortion and the Conscience of the Nation.* Nashville, TN: Thomas Nelson Publishers, 1984.

Rini, Suzanne M. *Beyond Abortion: A Chronicle of Fetal Experimentation,* Avon, NJ: Magnificat Press, 1988, republished by TAN Books and Publishers, Inc., Rockford, IL in 1993.

Shettles, Landrum B., M.D., and David Rorvik. *Rites of Life.* Grand Rapids, MI: Zondervan, 1983.

Siegel, Mark J., Patrick VonBrook, and Nancy R. Jacobs. *Abortion—An Eternal Social and Moral Issue.* Wylie, TX: Information Plus, 1990.

Storer, Horatio R. *On Criminal Abortion in America.* Philadelphia: Lippincott & Company, 1860.

Terry, Randall. *Operation Rescue.* Springdale, PA: Whitaker House, 1989.

Willke, John, M.D., and Mrs. *Abortion. . . Questions and Answers.* Cincinnati: Hayes Publishing, 1985.

Newspaper Articles

Abramowitz, Michael. "153 Arrested in Abortion Protest at D.C. Clinic." *Washington Post,* Jan. 24, 1989.

Boyd, Gerald. "Bush, in Iowa, Clarifies Stance on Legal Abortions." *New York Times,* Oct. 7, 1988.

"Change State Abortion Laws?" *USA Today,* July 7, 1989.

Clendinen, Dudley. "The Abortion Conflict: What It Does to One Doctor." *New York Times Magazine,* Aug. 11, 1985.

Cornell, George W. "Protestants Modify Stance on Abortion." *Herald-Mail,* Aug. 5, 1989.

DeSimone, Rev. Russell. "St. Augustine, Too, Opposed Abortion." *New York Times,* March 29, 1986.

Dujardin, Richard. "Prison Term Fails to Crush Resolve of Pro-Life Activist." *Washington Times,* Dec. 13, 1988.

Edwards, Jim. "Ultrasound Videotape Shows Unborn in Death Throes." *The Union Leader,* Nov. 20, 1984.

Erlandson, Greg. "Church Authorities Clarify Legal Definition of Abortion." *Arlington Catholic Herald,* Dec. 1, 1988.

Gorney, Cynthia. "Court Gives Woman Custody of 7 Embryo Children." *Washington Post,* Sept. 22, 1989.

"Geneticist Says Embryos Are 'Tiny Human Beings.'" *Washington Times,* Aug. 11, 1989.

Meehan, Mary. "The Ex-Abortionists: They Have Confronted the Reality." *Washington Post,* April 1, 1988.

Park, Robert, M.D. "Alcohol Can Cause Problems During Pregnancy." *Germantown* (MD) *Gazette,* Apr. 12, 1989.

Price, Joyce. "March for Life Attracts 65,000." *Washington Times,* Jan. 24, 1989.

Scully, Matthew. "Abortion Protest Attracts Thousand." *Washington Times,* Feb. 27, 1989.

"Stern Words by the Pope on Abortion." *New York Times,* Sept. 20, 1987, p. 31.

Thomas, Cal (syndicated columnist for the *Los Angeles Times*). "Pro-Life Forces on the Offensive." Printed in the *Washington Times,* Aug. 29, 1988.

Thompson, Morris. "Atlanta Police Use Tougher Tactics as Abortion Foes Return to Streets." *Washington Post,* Oct. 5, 1988.

Films

Eclipse of Reason. American Portrait Films. Anaheim, CA.
Massacre of Innocence. Reel to Real Ministries. Gainesville, FL.
The Silent Scream. American Portrait Films. Anaheim, CA.

Brochures

Paul Rockwell, M.D. "Consider This Observation by a New York Doctor." Pregnancy Center brochure, 1988.

Melody Green. "Children... Things We Throw Away?" Lyndale, TX: Pretty Good Printing, 1986.

Other Periodicals

"A Man's Viewpoint on Abortion." *Great Expectations,* Fall 1988, Newsletter of the Rockville (MD) Pregnancy Center.

Destro, Robert A. "Abortion and the Constitution: The Need for a Life-Protective Amendment." *California Law Review* 63 (1975): 1250, 1286.

Fairfax, Olga. "101 Uses for a Dead (or Alive) Baby." *ALL About Issues,* Jan., 1984.

Howard, Jacob M. *Congressional Globe,* Vol. 36, Washington, D.C., May 23, 1866.

Liley, A. W. "The Foetus as a Personality." *Australia and New Zealand Journal of Psychiatry,* Vol. 6, No. 2 (June 1972).

"So Says John Calvin." *Great Expectations* (Fall edition, Newsletter of the Rockville Pregnancy Center). Rockville, Maryland, 1988.

Tisdale, Sallie. "We Do Abortions Here." *Harper's Magazine,* October, 1987.

Valman, H. B., and J. F. Pearson. "What the Fetus Feels." *The British Medical Journal,* Jan. 26, 1980.

Laws and Other Legal Material

United States

Akron v. Akron Center for Reproductive Health. 462 U.S. 416.
Byrn v. New York City Health and Hospitals Corp. 31 N.Y. 2d 207.
Code of Virginia. 1849.
Compiled Statutes of Virginia. 1854.
Federal Register, Vol. 53, No. 21. Feb. 2, 1988.
Irish Constitution, "Eighth Amendment of the Constitution Act." Ireland: 1983.
Re Friday's Estate. 313 Pa. 328, 1933.
Roe v. Wade. 410 U.S. 113 (1973).
Thornburgh v. American Coll. of Obst. & Gyn. 476 U.S. 747.
Title X as cited in *Federal Register,* Vol. 53, No. 21. Feb. 2, 1988.
U.K. Statutes at Large. Vol. 1, London: 1804.
U.K. Statutes at Large. Vol. 2, London: 1829.
Webster v. Reproductive Health Services. 109 S. Ct. 3040 (1989).

GIVE COPIES OF THIS BOOK, BECAUSE...

If the fetus is a human being, then abortion is the killing of a human being.

If innocent human beings are being legally killed in our country through abortion—and at least 1,500,000 abortions per year are being performed—then our nation (to say nothing of the world) is indeed deeply involved in the shedding of innocent blood.

And the Bible tells us that innocent blood cries out to God for vengeance. (*Genesis* 4:10).

Therefore, it is absolutely imperative 1) that the slaughter of these innocents be stopped; 2) that reparation be made to God for our past sins; and 3) that our nation embark on a life in accord with God's law; thus, 4) that God will no longer have *this* reason to withhold His graces from us as a society, to say nothing of withholding the answers needed to straighten out our severe social problems.

Is the Fetus Human clears away any doubt that the fetus IS human, thus bringing everyone's thinking to the first step: recognition of the fact that with abortion, the slaughter of innocents is taking place in our country and in the world.

Is the Fetus Human is the perfect book to awaken minds and hearts to the calamity that is going on right in our midst. Calmly bringing together a wealth of evidence, it will convince anyone who has an open mind. Simple and logical, it is perfect for students, as well as for doctors, journalists, radio talk-show hosts, teachers, professors, lawyers, young women, young men—and for all, because the terrible scourge of abortion is worldwide.

Therefore, we are making this book available at the lowest possible prices for widespread distribution to as many people as possible. The issue is the salvation of souls and peace in the world.

QUANTITY DISCOUNT

1 copy	5.00			
5 copies	3.00	each	15.00	total
10 copies	2.75	each	27.50	total
25 copies	2.50	each	62.50	total
50 copies	2.25	each	112.50	total
100 copies	2.00	each	200.00	total

Priced low purposely for wide distribution!

U.S. & CANADIAN POST./HDLG: If order totals $1-$5, add $1; $5.01-$10, add $2; $10.01-$30.00, add $3; $30.01-$50, add $4; $50.01-up, add $5.

Check, Visa, MasterCard, or Discover accepted.

TAN BOOKS AND PUBLISHERS, INC.
P.O. Box 424, Rockford, Illinois 61105
Call Toll Free: 1-800-437-5876

Great Pro-Life Books!!. . .

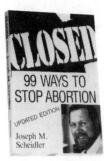

Pro-Life Books for All!! . . .

PRO-LIFE CHRISTIANS—Heroes for the Pre-born.

Joe Gulotta. Here are fascinating short stories of 28 Christians fighting abortion in a great variety of ways, covering just about every facet of the Pro-Life Movement. Positive, inviting and full of personal experience stories, this book has a can't-put-it-down style that keeps people reading on and on. Includes Carol Everett—former abortion-mill owner; Gianna Jessen—abortion survivor; Julie Makimaa—conceived through rape; Randall Terry—founder of "Operation Rescue"; Joan Andrews (Bell)—famous Rescuer; Sheriff James Hickey; Ultrasonographer Shari Richard; Gov. Robert Casey; and many more. Inspiring and encouraging! (5—4.00 ea.; 10—3.50 ea.; 15—3.25 ea.; 25—3.00 ea.; 100—2.75 ea.; 500—2.50 ea.; 1,000—2.25 ea.).

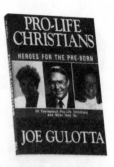

No. 1189. 146 pp. PB.
31 Illus.
ISBN-0-89555-460-7

7.00
(Prices guaranteed thru 12/31/94.)

No. 1217. 89 pp. PB.
3 Illus.
ISBN-0-89555-486-0

5.00
(Prices guaranteed thru 12/31/94.)

IS THE FETUS HUMAN?

Eric Pastuszek. In this enlightening and easy-to-read book is a variety of evidence—biological, medical, emotional, legal, cultural and social—showing that the fetus of a human mother is indeed human! Includes personal testimonies from women who have had abortions, from would-be fathers, from ex-abortionists and other medical personnel, plus tells how the pre-born infant can see, hear, jump, turn summersaults, suck its thumb and feel—all at a very early age. Also includes several remarkable photographs of fetal infants aborted but expelled from the womb "whole," leaving no doubt in either mind or heart that these children were, indeed, members of our own human race. An evocative book if ever there were one! (5—3.00 ea.; 10—2.75 ea.; 25—2.50 ea.; 50—2.25 ea.; 100—2.00 ea.).

U.S. & CANADIAN POST./HDLG: If order totals $1-$5, add $1; $5.01-$10, add $2; $10.01-$30.00, add $3; $30.01-$50, add $4; $50.01-up, add $5.

CALL TOLL FREE: 1-800-437-5876

TAN BOOKS AND PUBLISHERS, INC.
P.O. Box 424, Rockford, Illinois 61105

Both Facts and Inspiration!!...

No. 0139. 32 pp. PB.
7 Illus.
ISBN-0-89555-117-9

1.50

*(Prices guaranteed
thru 12/31/94.)*

ABORTION: YES OR NO? John L. Grady, M.D. Brief, clear and thorough, this little book refutes all arguments for abortion. It covers "medical indications" for abortion, "psychiatric indications," "fetal indications," the "mother's right to abortion," criminal abortion, abortion as a lucrative business, the humanity of the preborn child, and what abortion leads to. Includes methods of abortion, the history of the media's promotion of abortion and statements from authorities in various fields, then tells what we can do to work against abortion. Clear and direct, this book presents its punch without a wasted word. 420,000 sold! (5—1.00 ea.; 10—.80 ea.; 25—.75 ea.; 50—.60 ea.; 100—.50 ea.; 500—.45 ea.; 1,000—.40 ea.).

THE LIFE OF BLESSED MARGARET OF CASTELLO. Fr. William Bonniwell, O.P. Bl. Margaret (1287-1320) makes a great patroness for the Pro-Life Movement. She was born hunchbacked, midget, blind, lame and facially deformed. At a tender age her proud, noble parents walled her up beside a chapel. She could not get out, but could attend Mass and receive the Sacraments. After 14 years, her parents took her to a shrine to pray for a cure. No cure being forthcoming, they abandoned Margaret. She became a lay Dominican, performed miracles, and died at 33. Her incredible story is one of the most moving we have read. Her body remains incorrupt today.

No. 0202. 113 pp. PB.
9 Illus. Impr.
ISBN-0-89555-213-2

6.00

*(Prices guaranteed
thru 12/31/94.)*

U.S. & CANADIAN POST./HDLG: If order totals $1-$5, add $1; $5.01-$10, add $2; $10.01-$30.00, add $3; $30.01-$50, add $4; $50.01-up, add $5.

CALL TOLL FREE: 1-800-437-5876

**TAN BOOKS AND PUBLISHERS, INC.
P.O. Box 424, Rockford, Illinois 61105**

About the Author

Born near Philadelphia, Eric Pastuszek was educated in private schools; in 1985 he graduated *cum laude* from the University of Scranton with a double major in English and journalism. During his college tenure, he became editor of the university's literary magazine. Mr. Pastuszek now works in the field of technical writing for computers. He has received two awards for his work, and his knowledge of computers has helped him to understand the powerful advances of modern technology. However, he also sees man's loss of absolute truth within our highly technical society.

Mr. Pastuszek has given a powerful, objective look at this ironic denial of truth as related to the pre-born. In addition to his family responsibilities, he has taken time to research and write this concise but very compelling book.